Georgii Krutikov

The Flying City and Beyond

Selim Omarovich Khan-Magomedov

Translated by Christina Lodder

TENOV BOOKS

The first publication in Russian was released in Russia under the title 'Georgy Krutikov' by the author S.O. Khan-Magomedov, © ABCdesign, 2008.

This English translation published in September 2015.
© of this edition:
Editorial Tenov
Casp 147
08013 Barcelona
tenov@editorialtenov.com
www.tenovbooks.com

© of the translation: Christina Lodder

Design by TENOV and Hector Aspano

Cover image: Krutikov, 'The City of the Future (The Evolution of Architectural Principles in Town Planning and Residential Organisation)'. 1928. Fragment of a research work. Schusev State Museum of Architecture Collection, Moscow.

Printed in Norprint, Barcelona

ISBN: 978-84-939231-8-1
DL: B-17904-2015

Published with the support of the Institute for Literary Translation, Russia.

ИНСТИТУТ ПЕРЕВОДА

AD VERBUM

CONTENTS

Georgii Krutikov,
photograph.

A SENSATION AT THE VKHUTEMAS
(INSTEAD OF AN INTRODUCTION)

It was 1928. The Vkhutemas (Vysshie khudozhestvenno-tekhnicheskie masterskie: Higher Artistic and Technical Studios) was in uproar. For several years a tacit competition had existed between the diploma projects executed in the Architecture Faculty by students working in the studios of the leaders of the two fundamental creative trends of the architectural avant-garde of the 1920s – Aleksandr Vesnin (Constructivism) and Nikolai Ladovskii (Rationalism). Having gained a convincing victory in the Vkhutemas (from 1927 it was called the Vkhutein:Vysshii kudozhestvenno-tekhnicheskii institute: the Highher Artistic and Technical Institute), the avant-garde movements were now training qualified teams of their own supporters.

During the 1920s, the Vkhutemas-Vkhutein produced many talented architects, whose names are closely associated with the creative achievements of Soviet avant-garde architecture. The Vkhutemas was not only a unique complex of artistic educational institutions, but it was also one of the most important centres for the development of a new artistic style (above all in the sphere of architecture and design). The students' course and diploma project designs, which were published in the Soviet and foreign architectural press, played an important role in the creative experimentation and consolidation of the architectural avant-garde. In general, amongst these designs, the most interesting were those produced by Vesnin and Ladovskii's students.

In 1925, for instance, Andrei Burov, Vesnin's student, was awarded a study trip abroad on the basis of his brilliant diploma design for a railway station. The following year, Ladovskii's student, Mikhail Korzhev produced a marvellous diploma project for a sports stadium. In 1927, Ivan Leonidov, working with Vesnin, designed The Lenin Institute, which was widely acclaimed as a creative innovation. In 1928, Vitalii Lavrov and Trifon Varentsov's famous project, 'The New Cities', supervised by Ladovskii, was one of the diploma designs produced in the studios of Vesnin and Ladovskii that attracted particular attention.

The time for evaluating the 1928 diploma projects was already past, and both students and teachers were getting ready for the summer vacation, but one project remained unexamined. This unusually delayed examination was awaited with enormous interest. Nobody knew definitely what Georgii Krutikov's project looked like, nor its subject. Krutikov was one of Ladovskii's favourite students and the creative leader of Ladovskii's so-called charioteers (Krutikov, Lavrov, Sergei Lopatin and Valentin Popov), who opposed the followers of the Neo-Classicist Ivan Zholtovskii (Georgii Golts, Mikhail Parusnikov, Ivan Sobolev and Sergei Kozhin). The most contradictory rumours circulated.

Even the teachers knew very little about the details of Krutikov's project, despite the fact that students were only allowed to start work on the final version of their diploma designs after the Architecture Faculty of the Vkhutemas-Vkhutein had conducted a preliminary scrutiny of the projects. At that point, the committee had approved Krutikov's subject 'A City Plan'. Nevertheless, nobody had seen any of Krutikov's studies during his work on the project. The time came for the drawings to be submitted to the committee, a process that all students underwent before starting the final work on their diploma designs. Krutikov alone had not presented his sketches, having explained that he was not yet ready. Eventually, a final date was set for Krutikov to show the committee his diploma drawings.

Krutikov's drawings underwent a preliminary examination by a committee comprising Ladovskii himself, Nikolai Dokuchaev, Pavel Novitskii, Ilya Golosov, Ivan Rylskii, Konstantin Melnikov, Aleksandr Vesnin, Leonid Vesnin, Moisei Ginzburg, Yakov Raikh and others. The examination was held in Ladovskii's psycho-technical laboratory, which had black walls, ceiling and floor. In the centre of this room, Krutikov had placed cuttings from various journals on six tables, which were arranged in a U shape. He stood in the middle of this area, while the members of the committee moved freely from table to table, listening to his explanations.

It must be acknowledged that the most interesting diploma projects at the Vkhutemas-Vkhutein were not just professionally executed designs for a specific object, but were also conceived as creative solutions to a particular problem. For this reason, many of the designs were accompanied by sketches and models, relating to the specific subject of the exercise, which included a fairly broad theoretical component.

Georgii Krutikov,
photograh

Usually, the problem was analysed graphically and this included an extensive use of various types of visual material, plans and diagrams.

What Krutikov showed the members of the committee were the illustrations for the analytical component of his project. The illustrations were systematically displayed on the tables and included images of various types of transport such as a wheelbarrow, a camel, a sledge, a motor car, and an aeroplane. This material illustrated Krutikov's idea that, in the course of its evolution, humanity has increased the speed at which it is able to move, and that these different forms of transportation have influenced architecture, particularly housing. Krutikov considered that the most recent forms of transport should be regarded as mobile architecture and, as such, they suggested a different way of approaching the problem of the relationship between architecture and the environment. They raised the question: would it ever become possible to detach housing and other buildings from the land? Would it be possible to free the large amount of land on which buildings now stood? For Krutikov, land was vital to human beings, above all, because it enabled them to create favourable conditions for people on Earth. Was it absolutely necessary, therefore, to cover it with buildings? The dispersal of human settlements throughout the world limited man's potential to use the land effectively in the interests of society as a whole.

Among the cuttings that Krutikov displayed on his tables were those containing statistical information concerning the world's population growth, the percentage of land covered by water, ice, deserts, etc. He argued that the amount of the world's land mass that was suitable for humanity's use was limited, and the rapid territorial expansion of the world's population would produce considerable difficulties in the future. At the same time, developments in transportation were allowing human beings to move about more easily – people already spent a fair amount of time in various modes of transport, sometimes sleeping, eating, and almost 'living' in them.

There were also clippings showing that for aeons human beings had been attracted to elevations in their local surroundings, from which distant horizons opened up. In addition, there was material devoted to proving that mountainous districts provided a more favourable environment for human beings in terms of health and technology (people lived longer in the mountains, there was less dust and fewer microbes in the air, etc).

Among the numerous items of information were concepts for ideal cities, from different periods in history. Krutikov placed particular emphasis on the limited space in contemporary large cities, and the various town-planning projects that were struggling with this problem and trying to solve it. Alongside the items of information on the tables were Krutikov's schemes, explaining his ideas in graphic form as they related to one or another group of illustrations.

Having taken the members of the committee around the tables, Krutikov then showed them some preparatory sketches, which depicted a city in the sky. These sketches were executed on various small sheets of paper and were drawn in ink. It was clear that having devoted most of his time to analysing the problem, Krutikov had not yet managed to develop his project to the stage where it would normally have been supported by actual designs. The members of the committee were undecided, because the deadline had already passed, and it was essential to make a decision concerning Krutikov's fate. They all waited for Ladovskii's reaction – after all Krutikov was his student, and Ladovskii was not only particularly esteemed by his fellow teachers, but he was also known for his straight talking and harsh criticism of students' course work and diploma projects.

Ladovskii took the floor, and first of all he spoke about Krutikov, assessing him very highly in his presence, which was rare. Ladovskii considered that Krutikov thought in a complex, profound and visionary way as an architect and as a town planner, regarding the city as a social phenomenon, related to the development of technology, culture, and human needs. The subject that Krutikov had tackled was enormous in its extent and dealt with profoundly complex problems, which involved the most diverse issues. Naturally, it was difficult for one person to solve all the aspects of this problem and, therefore, Krutikov had not managed to meet the deadline in working out his ideas to the point where they could be embodied in the drawings necessary for the exam. Ladovskii then proposed accepting all the material that Krutikov had presented as preparatory work for his diploma project. Ginzburg supported this. Rylskii,who was then deacon of the Architecture Faculty and wrote the minutes of the examination, proposed giving Krutikov a ten-day extension for presenting his final diploma project. This decision was recorded in the minutes.

Ten days was more or less enough time to allow Krutikov to finish the sketches. But it was physically impossible to finish all the drawings, plans, and the analytical components of the project to the required standard in a mere ten days.

After the members of the committee had left the laboratory and its tables of cuttings, Krutikov's friends and colleagues in ASNOVA (Assotsiatsiya novykh arkhitektorov: Association of New Architects), who had been waiting impatiently to learn the results of the exam, came in. One of the active members of this creative group and the leader of its youngest and most radical wing, Viktor Balikhin, announced that this diploma exam affected ASNOVA's honour and therefore concerned not only Krutikov, but all the members of the group. At this brief meeting, it was decided that Krutikov should devote his energies to perfecting the analytical aspect of the project and working up the drawings, while the actual designs would be executed under his guidance by himself and his friends, Balikhin, Mikhail Korzhev, Mikhail Turkus, Nikolai Travin, Andrei Bunin and others.

The results of the committee's scrutiny of Krutikov's sketches had been widely publicised within the Vkhutein and had aroused a great deal of interest about the coming examination. On the day of the exam, many arrived early, long before it was to begin. People took their places noisily, sitting on window sills and tables.

But strangely, amid all the sensation preceding the examination, the person who was least concerned about this anticipated event, which was so important for the rest of his life, was the person responsible for the occasion. During the final days just before the examination, when his only aim should have been to perfect his drawings for the project, he continued to devote a lot of his attention to the general problem of the city of the future.

Krutikov differed from his peers in not paying a great deal of attention to current issues and everyday problems. His friends recall him being 'a thoughtful man' who often pondered questions that seemed to be remote from people's actual needs.

At this time, the Vkhutemas was almost like a debating society – violent arguments broke out and groups were formed and dissolved. In this situation, a significant role among the students was played by those who participated actively in the discussions. Krutikov was a shy and retiring young man with a spiritual face, who was never one of the recognised leaders, and wasn't a popular figure. Looking like a typical Russian peasant with a good-hearted smile, he was exceptionally straightforward and gentle in his relations with people. Beneath this simple exterior, his subtle mind, real intelligence and inner wisdom were not immediately apparent. He only revealed himself completely to those close to him. His friends recall that within their own circle he was considered exceptional.

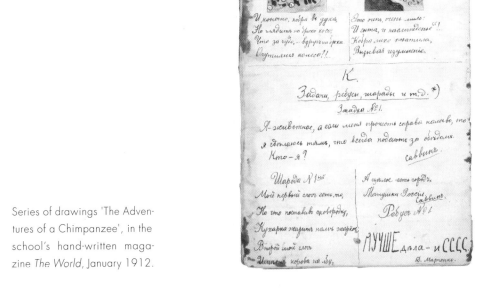

Series of drawings 'The Adventures of a Chimpanzee', in the school's hand-written magazine *The World*, January 1912.

Georgii Tikhonovich Krutikov was born in 1899 in the city of Voronezh into a family of teachers. His artistic talents were already apparent while he was still at school, where there was a very good art teacher (Sazonov). At the gymnasium, Krutikov's drawings received a lot of attention and were highly valued. They were even sent to an exhibition in Moscow, but unfortunately were never returned, to Krutikov's deep regret.

Krutikov's archive contains material from his schooldays which testifies to his two main interests – painting and space travel.

With regards to painting, there are two hand-written magazines, published by the school's younger pupils:

1) *All over the World* (*Po vsemu svetu*, No. 1, January-February 1911) a publication about science, literature and art; and
2) *The World* (*Svet*, No. 1, January 1912) an artistic and literary magazine. Krutikov contributed to both publications, as an author and as an artist.

Judging from his drawings for *The World*, in 1912, the twelve-year-old was not familiar with 'avant-garde' painting. The series of painterly illustrations for 'The Adventures of a Chimpanzee' (an original comic strip of fourteen drawings), was executed in a realistic manner.

In addition, his archive contains some undated theatrical works, which are also in a realistic idiom – designs for a set (The Prince's Bedroom) and costumes (male and female characters for Gentlemen), as well as a poster advertising the Experimental Theatrical Studio.

These works suggest that, as an artist, Krutikov only began to be attracted to avant-garde painting in 1914, when he was fifteen years old. Some of the drawings and paintings were executed in a Cubist style: the *Portrait of a Man, Still Life with Jug, Landscape with Church* (dated 1914), and *Cityscape.*

Still Life with Jug,
Cityscape, Portrait of a Man.

Designs for the theatrical set
design *The Prince's Bedroom*
and costumes for *Gentlemen*.

Воздухоплаваніе.

научная статья Г. Крутикова.

Историческій очеркъ.

Еще въ греческой миѳологіи, задолго до нашей эры, мы находимъ прекрасную легенду о смѣломъ юношѣ Икарѣ, освободившемся съ своихъ отцемъ изъ плѣна съ помощью придуманныхъ восковыхъ крыльевъ. Икаръ желалъ подлетѣть къ солнцу, но по приближеніи его къ свѣтилу, воскъ хрупкій растаялъ и юноша упалъ въ море...

Много вѣковъ прошло до тѣхъ поръ, когда мечтанія грековъ стали осуществляться.

Лѣтомъ 1783 года во франц. уѣздѣ городѣ Аноно, фабриканты бумаги, братья Монгольфьеръ изобрѣли большой шаръ — аэростатъ — съ подвѣшанной къ нему

площадкой, гдѣ разводился огонь. Воздухъ, входившій въ шаръ, нагрѣвался, и шаръ отдѣлялся отъ земли такъ, какъ нагрѣтый воздухъ, который легче холоднаго, поднималъ аэростатъ.

Шаръ летѣлъ туда, куда его относилъ вѣтеръ. Полеты поэтому были сопряжены съ большой опасностью и нерѣдко кончались катастрофами.

Такъ, въ 1785 году погибъ смѣлый авіаторъ Пилатеръ-де-Розье, пытавшійся пролетѣть черезъ проливъ Ла-Маншъ. Это было въ концѣ XVIII вѣка.

Послѣ длиннаго ряда попытокъ усовершенствовать аэростатъ Монгольфьеровъ, съ цѣлью достичь возможно болѣе безопаснаго полета по воздуху, на ... нашли возможность надувать шаръ особеннымъ газомъ, водородомъ,

значительно болѣе легкимъ чѣмъ воздухъ. ... и фр. ... въ 1852 году, Дюнви-делъ ... братья Тиссандье въ 1883 году ... приставлять къ подобнымъ шарамъ различные механизмы, для того, чтобы подчинить аэростатъ своей волѣ, но все-таки все, въ сущности, оставалось по прежнему, — шаръ былъ вполнѣ подчиненнымъ воздуху. Но гдѣ настойчивость ... и побѣда. И, наконецъ, упорныя усилія приводятъ къ несомнѣнному успѣху. Въ 1884 году, около Парижа поднимается управляемый аэростатъ, построенный офицерами ... Кребсомъ и Ренаромъ. На лодочкѣ, подвѣшанной къ шару надутому водородомъ, былъ установленъ довольно тяжелый электрическій двигатель съ винтомъ, очень охотно съ паровою ... Благодаря быстрому враще...

его и различнымъ воздушнымъ рулямъ, этотъ шаръ описывалъ въ воздухѣ на значительной высотѣ кругъ и благополучно опускается... Но долго онъ летать не могъ, такъ какъ моторъ его особенно тяжелъ и слабосиленъ.

Г. Крутиковъ.

(продолженіе слѣдуетъ)

Изъ обычаевъ Китая.

Отчего у китайцевъ мода уродовать ноги женщинамъ?

Мы всѣ знаемъ, что въ Китаѣ женщинамъ уродуютъ ноги съ самыхъ раннихъ лѣтъ; чѣмъ меньше нога, тѣмъ женщина считается красивѣе. Операція, при помощи которой можно достигнуть это, довольно непріятна; когда нога дѣвочки представляется ... ея забинтовываютъ крѣпкой повязкой, такъ что

While still in the youngest class at the gymnasium, Georgii Krutikov had become interested in the problem of aeronautics. At the beginning of the twentieth century, it was not yet clear what form air transport would take in the future – the aeroplane or the airship. At that time, many considered that the aeroplane would be best for military activities (this was subsequently confirmed during the First World War). For passenger air travel, the preferred mode was the airship, to which gondolas (passenger cabins) were attached. The terrible airship accidents of the 1930s had not yet happened, and many people still believed that the future of aeronautics lay with the airships, as the successors to the hot-air balloons.

In 1911, the twelve-year-old Georgii Krutikov published an article entitled 'Aeronautics (An Historical Report)' in the hand-written school magazine. It was, of course, a naïve, almost childish article. Yet I think that it is useful to reprint it here in full, because it relates directly and clearly to the future problems on which Krutikov worked and which led him to develop the project of 'The Flying City' – the main work of his life. The article was written by hand and was accompanied by small drawings of the Montgolfier brothers' hot-air balloon, an aerostat (a moored balloon), and an airship.

G. Krutikov, 'Aeronautics (An Historical Report)'.

In Greek mythology, long before our times, we find the wonderful legend of the brave young man Icarus, fleeing prison with his father and using wings attached with wax. Icarus wanted to fly to the sun, but as he approached it, the wax on the wings melted and the young man fell into the sea.

Many centuries passed before the dreams of the Greeks were realised.

In summer 1783, in the French town of Annonay, the Montgolfier brothers, who were paper manufacturers, invented a large balloon – an **aerostat**, to which a platform was attached, on which a fire was burning.

The air entering the balloon was heated, and the balloon left the ground, because the hot air, which is lighter than cold air, lifted it.

The balloon flew wherever it was blown by the wind. Flights were, therefore, accompanied by great danger and often ended in disaster.

In this way, in 1785, the brave aviator Planer-de-Rozier [Pilâtre de Rozier] was killed, trying to cross the English Channel. This was at the end of the eighteenth century.

After a long series of attempts to improve the Montgolfiers' balloon and make flying less dangerous, it was discovered that the balloon could be inflated with a special gas, hydrogen, which was substantially lighter than air. In 1852 Giffard with [Julien?], and in 1883 the Tissandbe [Tissandier] brothers tried to attach different mechanisms to these balloons in order to make the balloon submit to their control, but in reality, the situation remained more or less as before – the balloon was completely at the mercy of the wind. Perseverance, however, leads to victory. Ultimately, persistent efforts resulted in undoubted success. In 1884, near Paris a controllable dirigible, built by the officers Krebs and Renard, was flown. In the basket, hanging from the balloon, which was filled with hydrogen, there was a fairly heavy electric motor with a screw mechanism, just like that on a steam ship. Thanks to its rapid revolutions and various air rudders, this balloon was able to describe a circle at a significant height and land successfully... But it could not fly for long because the motor was too heavy and weak (to be continued).[1]

As we can see, Krutikov was seriously interested in the problems of aeronautics and intended to provide the hand-written journal with a series of articles, calling them initially 'scientific articles', but then modestly reducing their status to that of 'historical reports'.

After leaving school in 1917, the eighteen-year-old Krutikov worked in Voronezh as the secretary of the Fine Art Section of the city's Education Department, and then as head of the Art Sub-Section of the Regional Education Department. In his capacity as an artist-decorator, he designed productions for the Experimental Theatrical Studio. At the same time, he worked on organising the Voronezh State Free Art Educational Studios.

The Handbook of the Art Department of the Commissariat for Enlightenment (Moscow, 1920) lists various 'State Free Art Training Studios' and includes the following paragraph: 'Voronezh: 3 Painting studios; 1 Decorative studio. Representative: Krutikov.'[2]

Studies for posters for the Voronezh Institute of Theatrical Art (The Theatrical Department of the Chief Administration for Vocational Training) and the Voronezh Higher State Artistic and Technical Workshops (The Art Department of the Chief Administration for Vocational Training).

In 1922, Krutikov moved to Moscow to enter the Vkhutemas and continue his education. Krutikov's widow Klavdiya Vasilevna Krutikova, in conversation with me in 1971, described how she had met her husband in 1918 and that at first he had wanted to be an artist, but his family's opposition to this influenced him, so at the Vkhutemas, he immediately enrolled in the Architecture Faculty where he studied with Nikolai Ladovskii.

While a student at the Vkhutemas, Krutikov, as in Voronezh, continued to be intensely interested in aeronautics. His archive contains numerous cuttings of all kinds from newspapers and magazines related to the subject. He was interested in both trends in the development of aeronautics – aeroplanes and airships. He worked on a course project for an aeroplane factory, and bought and read the journal *Aeroplane* (*Samolet*).

Nevertheless, in the mid 1920s, his main interest was airships. Krutikov paid particular attention to the development of the airship's gondola and developed his own ideas about designing its interior as a complex architectural space. This is indicated by several drawings in his archive. He also worked on this problem with El Lissitzky, a fellow member of ASNOVA. Krutikov even wrote a letter about his ideas concerning the architectural development of the gondola to the rocket scientist Konstantin Tsiolkovskii. [3]

Unfortunately, there is very little information about Krutikov's work on the design for the airship gondola and his possible contacts with Tsiolkovskii. Only two items of documentary evidence exist. The first fact: in *ASNOVA News* (*Izvestiya ASNOVA*, 1926), the page concerning information about the group's work contains the following paragraph: '2. The section of transport architecture. Work is being conducted on the architectural design of Tsiolkovskii's airship (Lissitzky and Krutikov in collaboration with the engineer Vinogradov)'.[4] The second fact: in January 1926, Krutikov wrote in a letter to his wife: 'I have finished with the airship for the time being and have passed it over to Lissitzky for completion. I am now concentrating on the aeroplane factory.' [i.e. his course project – Khan-Magomedov].

p. 24–25: Exhibition of Work by Students of the Voronezh State Free Art Educational Studios, which Krutikov helped to organise.

Course project design for an aeroplane factory. Façade, axonometric projection, plan, and cross-section. 1926.

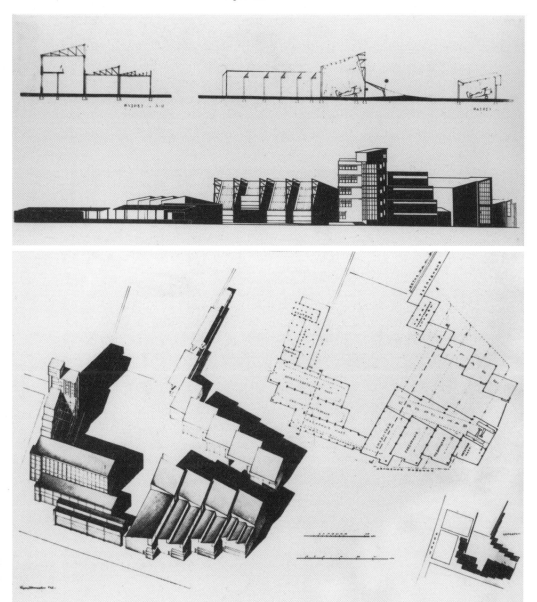

Studies for a design for an airship's gondola or passenger cabin. Façade, cross-section, perspective and plans.

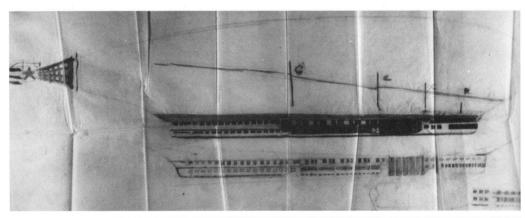

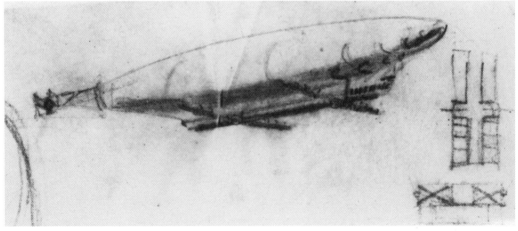

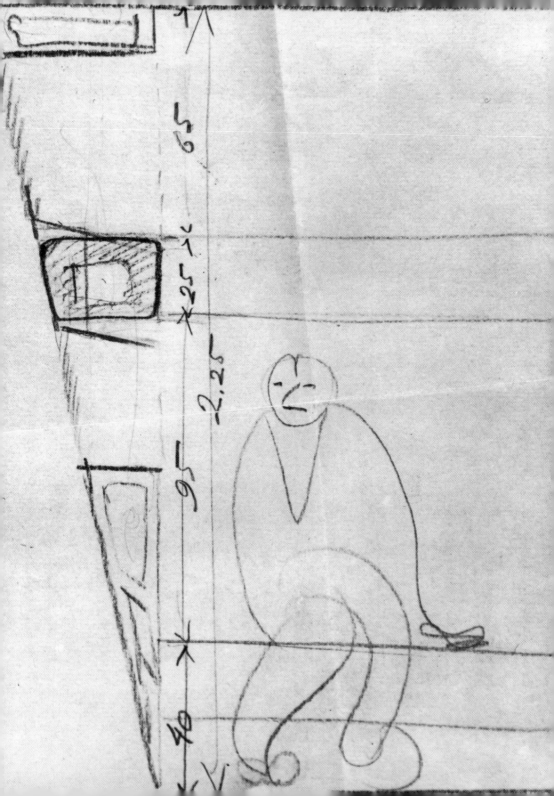

Article from the French magazine *l'Illustration* presenting Lecuyer and Jubault's project for a rotating house.

La villa *Tournesol*, d'après la maquette exposée à Nice.
MM. Georges Lécuyer et Henri Jubault, architectes ; M. Lucien Boudot, décorateur.

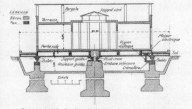

Coupe montrant la disposition des fondations et du système giratoire.
La coupe étant faite par le centre de l'atrium, on n'aperçoit pas l'étage qui recouvre seulement le vestibule.

UNE MAISON TOURNANTE

Bien avant qu'Edmond Rostand chantât son hymne au soleil, l'architecte des Ptolémées inscrivait au fronton du temple de Philæ :

C'est lui, le soleil, qui fait tout ce qui est. Et rien n'a été fait sans lui jamais.

Tous, nous admirons le soleil, nous reconnaissons ses bienfaits et nous croyons l'aimer. Amour assez relatif ; car autant nous le souhaitons quand il est loin, quand il se hasarde royalement à transfigurer pendant quelques heures une journée d'hiver, autant nous nous empressons à le fuir quand, dans la plénitude de sa puissance, il exalte la splendeur des jours d'été. Il est cependant des hommes qui, en période de canicule, aiment sa chaleur bienfaisante et la couleur de sa lumière ; il en est aussi qui, durant les quelques mois où il assure les douceurs de l'hiver et du printemps de notre Méditerranée, voudraient, depuis son lever jusqu'à son coucher, vivre avec lui.

Tel dut être le sentiment de deux architectes parisiens, MM. Georges Lécuyer et Henri Jubault, qui, dans une heure de loisir ou de rêverie, si ce n'est un jour de brume, ont imaginé la villa *Tournesol*, villa tournante, orientable à volonté, dont une maquette très étudiée est peut-être le clou de l'Exposition de l'habitation et des arts décoratifs qui vient de s'ouvrir à Nice. Véritable joujou de multimillionnaire, cette villa ne rappelle en rien les maisonnettes des bergeries de Nuremberg ; elle constitue une habitation complète, confortable et spacieuse. Malgré la nouveauté et la hardiesse de sa conception, elle vaut d'être prise au sérieux.

Ce home repose sur un plateau mobile en métal et béton armé qui rappelle un peu les plaques tournantes des gares, mais qui présente des dispositifs spéciaux en raison du poids de la construction, très supérieur à celui des wagons et même à celui d'une locomotive moderne. Le plateau est formé par huit poutres rayonnantes assemblées sur un moyeu qui abrite le pivot central. Chaque poutre porte vers son extrémité un des huit galets en fonte dure qui supportent le poids de l'ensemble. Ces galets roulent sur un rail accroché à des fondations circulaires laissant entre elles et le plateau un vide suffisant pour la visite et l'entretien.

Le mécanisme de giration proprement dit est constitué par une crémaillère courbe installée sous le plateau et qu'attaque un pignon actionné par un moteur électrique. Il suffit de presser sur un bouton à l'intérieur de la maison pour mettre la maison en marche ou pour l'arrêter instantanément. Avec un moteur de 4 chevaux, la maison fait un tour à l'heure ; il suffit donc d'un petit quart d'heure pour rejoindre le soleil si on l'a laissé s'écarter d'un angle de 90 degrés. Cette vitesse paraît suffisante ; elle permet l'accès facile de la maison quand celle-ci se promène. Une difficulté assez grande était d'éviter les déplacements ou les coincements sous l'action d'un vent violent ; on l'a résolu en disposant au centre de la maison un fort pivot métallique avec galets à rouleaux.

Un des grands mérites de cette conception, au fond assez simple, mais que d'aucuns peuvent trouver révolutionnaire, est d'avoir été réalisé avec une sûreté de goût et avec une sobriété architecturale et décorative que l'on ne rencontre point toujours dans les fantaisies des modernistes. A la forme en rotonde, en apparence plus logique, les architectes ont préféré la forme polygonale, moins monotone, et dont les arêtes délimitent judicieusement les nus qu'égaient des motifs discrets sur fond d'or.

Pour cette décoration extérieure, comme pour tout l'aménagement intérieur, les architectes ont eu l'heureuse idée de s'adresser à un artiste éminent, M. Lucien Boudot, bien connu des amateurs de somptuosités par la science de l'harmonie des couleurs et par le tact, d'ailleurs plein d'originalité, avec lequel il traite les ensembles quand il s'éloigne des styles passés. Car M. Boudot ne dédaigne ni les boudoirs Louis XVI ni les salons Régence ; mais, tout en s'ingéniant à éviter le pastiche dans ses créations modernes, il ignore la préoccupation, trop souvent dominante aujourd'hui, de faire quelque chose « qui ne ressemble à rien ».

Habitués que nous sommes à des pièces plus ou moins rectangulaires, il nous paraît difficile au premier abord de « composer » agréablement pour l'œil, voire pour le confort, une pièce un peu en forme de V coupé. M. Boudot a très habilement tiré parti de cette forme originale ; il lui a suffi de distribuer judicieusement de pans coupés, autant fixes, sous forme d'une cloison aménageant un placard ; tantôt mobiles, sous forme d'une vitrine, d'un argentier ou de quelque autre meuble adapté au caractère et à la destination de la pièce. Comme beaucoup de ses confrères, il recourt aux bois du Gabon ; mais, aux taches brutales de couleur, si fort à la mode, il préfère les harmonies douces et claires qu'appelle le soleil et d'où le noir, dont on abuse, est sévèrement banni.

Voici, par exemple, une chambre où les tons chauds d'acajou drapé se marient à l'argent qui s'étale sur les sièges et qui vibre discrètement dans les plis des rideaux ou dans les motifs dont s'enrichissent les tentures mauves, — ensemble rêvé pour l'entrée du soleil levant. Dans le cabinet de travail, le palissandre met en valeur une combinaison de vert amande et de vieux jaune d'Utrecht que l'artiste a pris soin d'adopter aussi pour la reliure des livres qui apparaissent en lumière dans un effet d'unisson nouveau, absolument inédit.

La salle de bains, avec son revêtement de céramique fleur de pêcher, fera rêver bien des femmes, même pour une maison qui ne tournerait pas ; et l'on chercherait en vain la moindre nuance pompéienne dans l'atrium dont les murs en bleu Wedgwood s'accordent avec un dallage de marbre blanc et de marbre bleu turquin.

D'après un devis très serré, la villa Tournesol toute meublée reviendrait à peu près à 1.250.000 francs, soit à peine 200.000 francs d'avant-guerre. Dans ce prix, le mécanisme entre pour 200.000 francs. Un amateur riche, dans la mesure que représente aujourd'hui la richesse, pourra donc aisément s'offrir cette villa qui, abstraction faite de sa fantaisie giratoire, constitue un bel ensemble d'art et de mécanique moderne.

Ajoutons, pour consoler les déshérités relatifs de la fortune, que les auteurs du projet envisagent la possibilité d'établir des villas moins grandes et moins luxueuses, mais tout aussi tournantes, dont le mécanisme ne coûterait qu'une vingtaine de mille francs. En économisant un peu sur les détails, on pourrait donc, sans être très riche, s'offrir « pour rien » une maison qui tourne.

Après l'instinctive surprise qu'apporte l'idée d'une maison tournante, l'esprit s'habitue vite à cette réalisation ; on est même presque étonné de la voir apparaître si tard, car, par sa forme arrondie et son mouvement de rotation, elle est en parfaite harmonie avec la forme et le mouvement universels.

SÉROINE.

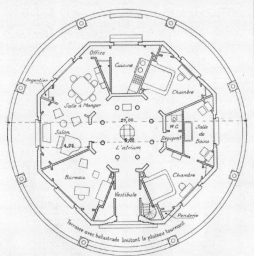

Plan de la villa sur sa plaque tournante.

TACKLING THE PROBLEM OF MOBILE ARCHITECTURE

One of Krutikov's first real architectural designs was a hostel for sportsmen, which was part of a collective entry to the competition concerning the design of the International Red Stadium complex in Moscow (1924). Krutikov's design already reveals his distinctive characteristics as an architect. He always tried to use at least one element (in a course project or an actual design) as a focus for defining or solving a particular creative problem. He did not consider that it was adequate to tackle a specific problem by merely relying on an established architectural syntax or using existing approaches and resources. He constantly attached additional problems to an individual task, and these usually related to an issue that arose from the framework of the project itself. Hence, in his design for the International Red Stadium hostel, Krutikov tried to develop a new type of living capsule, which was semi-circular in plan. Subsequently, he continued working on this living capsule, employing it in his pre-diploma project for an art college complex and conducting research, the results of which he published in his article 'Circular or Semi-Circular Housing' of 1927. Here is a fragment of that text:

> Recently the foreign press has devoted a lot of attention to 'Circular Houses'. The construction of the first circular house in Germany by Bruno Taut and the rotating house of the Parisian architects [Georges] Lecuyer and [Henri] Jubault caused a sensation.
>
> The motives inspiring the circular buildings of the Germans and the French are different. While Bruno Taut and Carl Fieger are interested in the circular form with respect to the most economic use of space and reducing the parameters of enclosing walls, the rotating house of Lecuyer and Jubault was built with the aim of 'catching' the sun.
>
> The sensational Villa Tournesol (The Sunflower House), which constantly turns to face the sun, ... is not concerned with economic construction. It has a different purpose. A four-horsepower engine determines its speed, which is approximately one rotation per hour. Hence a quarter of an hour

is enough to catch the sun, if it is at an angle of 90°. This speed also does not prevent free access to the house during its movement and is completely unnoticed by the house's occupants. The rotating apparatus consists of an electric clockwork mechanism which causes a specially constructed rotating circle to move with the assistance of cogs ...

... All these original houses and villas were essentially nothing other than detached residences for individuals.

... Therefore, as regards economics and everyday social life, they are of little interest to us, except for the revolving house, where the idea of movement *per se* is very interesting for further development. In this respect, this small villa presented a great stimulus to our imagination, providing a bridge between static architecture and an architecture of moving structures.[5]

Further on in the article, Krutikov publicised the semi-circular living capsule that he had developed in 1924, stressing its advantages in comparison with other types of living units. In his opinion:

the semi-circular cell is an extraordinarily flexible and advantageous element in the hands of architects when it is combined in various types of residences, from large individual houses to skyscrapers containing numerous apartments.

It allows an unlimited and, at the same time, simple accretion of storeys. It is light and can be easily combined into blocks, without altering its essential form. In this way, when regularised, it will make the widespread standardised construction of residential buildings possible.[6]

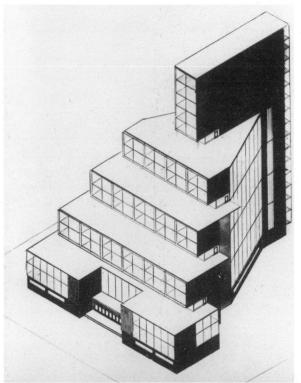

Pre-diploma project design at the Vkhutemas – A Higher Art College Complex (Nikolai Ladovskii's studio). Teaching block. Axonometric projection and model of the complex.

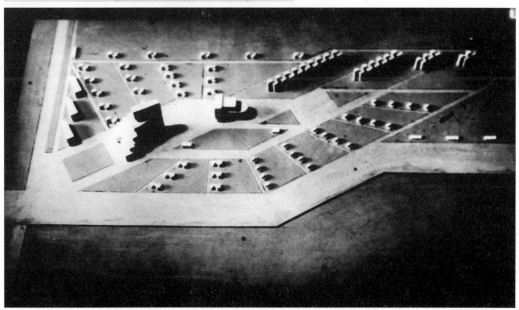

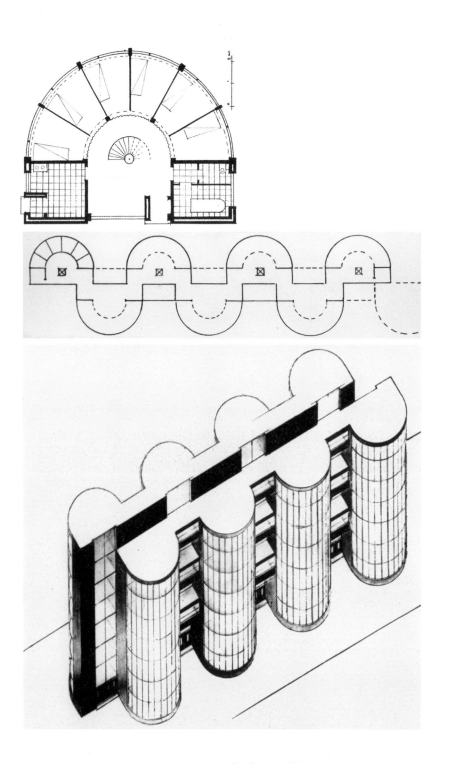

Pre-diploma project design at the Vkhutemas – A Higher Art College Complex (Nikolai Ladovskii's studio). Left: Student hostel. Ground plans and axonometric projection. Right: Houses for the teachers and staff. Axonometric projection, plans and cross-sections. 1927.

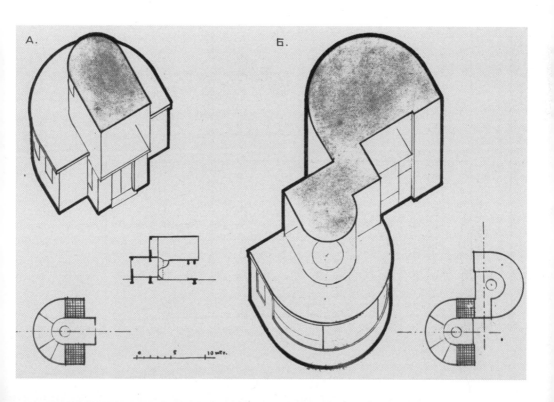

Personal Record Card for entering the results of the psycho-technical test for architectural talent.

Архитектурная
НАУЧНО-ИССЛЕДОВАТ.
Лаборатория
В. Х. Т. И.

Дата испытания .... №№ мат. ....

РЕЗУЛЬТАТЫ ИСПЫТАНИЯ

....

Внимание.		И	Р	К	Простр. одаренность.		И	Р	К
Память	1				Пр. координация				
Фигуры	2				вертикальн. . . .	14			
Угол	3				горизонтальн. . . .	15			
Ср. коэф. . . .					Ср. коэф.				
Глазомер.					Пр. ориентиров. .	16			
линия а	4.5				Пр. представл. .	17			
линия б.	6.7				Пр. воображен. .	18			
площадь	8.9				Пр. комбинирован.				
об'ем	10.11				тест 1, 2	19.20			
угол	12				„Альфа"	21			
ср. коэф.					Ср. коэф.				
Чувство отнош. . . .	13				Ср. коэф. по пр. одар.				
					Моторная одарени.				

(Психологический профиль архитектурной одаренности — graph grid with vertical scale 1–10 on left, 0–100 on right, horizontal axis labeled 1 2 3 4/5 6/7 8/9 10/11 12 13 14 15 16 17 18 19/20 21 22 В П Г О П м)

Общее заключение ....

Зав. лабораторией:

Категория ....

THE PSYCHO-TECHNICAL LABORATORY AT THE VKHUTEMAS

In 1927, Nikolai Ladovskii organised an architectural, scientific and experimental (psycho-technical) laboratory at the Vkhutein. Krutikov became one of Ladovskii's chief assistants in the work of the laboratory. The investigative character of Krutikov's talent and his tendency to develop or apply a new and unresolved problem to every project found extensive application in the work of the laboratory. He devoted a lot of time and energy to the laboratory, frequently sacrificing his academic work to the research he conducted there.

In the plan for the laboratory's scientific and experimental work, Krutikov included his own topic 'On the path towards a mobile architecture'. Defining the tasks of his research, Krutikov wrote that 'architecture is striving to become increasingly mobile. In future, obsolete and inconvenient town planning must be replaced by flexible planning, which is based on new principles of defining space. Helping to develop this new mobile architecture is the task of the present day and the vital business of the contemporary architect-inventor'.[7]

The psycho-technical laboratory opened on 15 February 1927. Material concerning its work during 1927 and 1928 was published in articles by Ladovskii's students – Krutikov and Vitalii Lavrov. This material is complemented by documents preserved in Krutikov's archive, including a signed report on the laboratory's work during the first year of its existence. In addition, I managed to talk to many of the former students and post-graduates at the Vkhutein, who were involved in the work of the laboratory or took examinations using its equipment: Andrei Bunin, Mikhail Barshch, Yulii Savitskii, Georgii Borisovskii, Gevorg Kochar, Mikhail Mazmanyan, Mikhail Sinyavskii, Petr Gubarev, Nikolai Krasilnikov, Viktor Kalmykov and others.

This is how Krutikov defined the fundamental purpose of the laboratory in one of his articles: 'The basic task of the Architectural Laboratory is to create a scientifically based and experimentally verified foundation which will be able to **refine** [emphasis – Khan-Magomedov] the present intuitive approach.'[8]

The laboratory's programme and activities were divided into the following three groups of problems:

1. The Section Concerning the Analysis of Architectural Elements

The general aim of the research was to establish the quantity and quality of the effects that the basic architectural elements had on the viewer, and to systematise these effects. The investigation was conducted along several lines:

a) Studying the immediate effect that forms, colours, volumes, spaces, etc., had on the psyche.
b) Investigating the general and particular properties of these elements.
c) Examining the interaction of form and colour, colour and space etc.
d) Exploring the effects of colour, light and texture on an architectural structure.
e) Conducting a comprehensive study and experimental examination of the spatial disciplines of the Vkhutein's Basic Course.
f) Probing and analysing the nature of composition (organic and non-organic, static and dynamic, etc).

2. The Organisational and Economic Section

Investigating the social and domestic as well as the technical and economic problems of architecture, including architectural sociology; architectural form and the environment; architecture and the new way of life; the influence of typification and standardisation on architectural practice; and the impact on architecture of the Scientific Organisation of Work (NOT – Nauchnaya organizatsiya truda).

3. The Pedagogical Section

Problems of defining the suitability of individuals for the profession of architecture, and investigating questions relating to the methods of teaching architectural subjects:

a) An architect's psycho-technics.
b) The elaboration of rational methods of teaching architectural design in a contemporary school of architecture.

In order not to disturb the concentration of the investigators and those being investigated, or create inessential reference points that would affect the results of the experiments, Ladovskii decided to paint the walls, floor and ceiling of his laboratory black. Apparently, the decorators refused to paint everything black, and Ladvoskii's assistants (including Krutikov) had to paint it. This 'Black Room' produced a fantastic impression on the visitor, crammed full, as it was, with all sorts of unusual apparatus with extended wires and brightly coloured spots, which were used for experiments with colour. One eyewitness recalls that when you entered the laboratory you got the feeling that there had just been a fire.

As Krutikov wrote in his report, in order to register authorship 'the laboratory records in a special book, and thus preserves, a description of the work produced by a researcher along with his signature'.

One can categorise the work included in the laboratory's plan during the time of its brief existence into the following groups:

1. Research conducted in the laboratory itself under Ladovskii's supervision, which included not only the theoretical elaboration of problems, but also experiments with appliances or models (examples of equipment), texts, questionnaires, etc. Among these I will mention only those to which Krutikov contributed, i.e. work connected with the psycho-technics of the architect and work on the experimental verification of the spatial disciplines.
2. Subjects developed personally by individual post-graduates or undergraduate students. Sometimes these subjects were initially developed outside the laboratory, and then absorbed into its work plan. Amongst these subjects was Krutikov's 'On the path towards a mobile architecture. Its social, technical and formal foundations'.

We will briefly examine those problems on which Krutikov worked, beginning with the psycho-technics of the architect. The laboratory set itself the task of helping to select students entering the Vkhutein's Architecture Faculty, and of assisting teachers with the process of teaching individual students and developing their necessary professional skills. The problem was that architecture was an area of expertise for which there did not yet exist any scientifically established criteria for evaluating a person's suitability for this particular kind of creative work. Krutikov wrote:

> The absence of any kind of scientific approach towards selecting suitable candidates for entrance to schools of architecture has been felt particularly acutely up till now. The existing view that an aptitude for drawing indicates a talent for art and hence for architecture must be regarded as entirely without any foundation. The ability to organise spatial forms bears no relation at all to the fine-art skills of depicting forms on a plane. Suffice it to recall that most sculptors have no talent for drawing. The peculiarity of this viewpoint, of course, has its foundation in the erroneous organisation of architectural education and training that was prevalent in the recent past. If the correct determining features for the concept of 'an architect' can be established, this will naturally be reflected in the quality of his work – his architecture.[9]

And here is another quotation from an article by Krutikov, where he explains in more detail why the problems of an architect's psycho-technical skills were considered to be so important in the work of the laboratory:

> 1. A detailed knowledge of all the elements of the mechanism that regulates the architect's working process is an essential basis for the scientific organisation of his work (architectural design).
>
> 2. Without a preliminary and adequate development of the problems relating to the psycho-technics of the architect, it is also impossible to establish an objective method for teaching architectural design (a vital issue in the contemporary school of architecture).
>
> 3. Exploring the psycho-technics of the architect is closely connected with the problem of efficiently organising the Architecture Faculty and with the question of professionally advising the student body.[10]

The laboratory's first practical task was to develop methods and systems for the psycho-technical selection of candidates entering the Vkhutein's Architecture Faculty. In the course of resolving this problem, research focused on the architect's working process, analysing that process into its constituent elements, and developing texts for defining the quantitative evaluation of the results of the experiments. The system of tests developed by the laboratory was essentially new. It reflected Ladovskii's ideas concerning the decisive role of space in the various elements of architectural expression. Everything was directed towards accurately assessing the 'spatial abilities' of the person being investigated. These were defined as skills in the field of spatial co-ordination (vertically and horizontally), spatial orientation, spatial perception, spatial imagination, and spatial combination.

As Krutikov wrote, 'factors of "spatial ability" occupied as central a place here as, for instance, the detection of a sense of equilibrium and an ability to balance has in the testing of pilots.'[11] The system developed in the laboratory was used to test students who were entering the Architecture Faculty of the Vkhutein in autumn 1928. The system consisted of two types of tests – one was conducted on a special device, the other on sheets of paper, which were prepared in advance and given to each candidate.

The laboratory apparatus that Ladovskii constructed intended to test and evaluate the eye's capabilities in relation to various properties of form and scale: the line (a *liglazometr* – a linear sight measure), the plane (*ploglazometr* – a planar sight measure), volume (*oglazometr* – a volumetric sight measure), angles (*uglazometr* – an angle sight measure) and space (*prostrometr* –a spatial sight measure).[12] These instruments were not merely used to test the student's visual abilities, but also to develop them.

In addition to the equipment for testing visual aptitude, the laboratory also possessed devices consisting of various forms and configurations of planar and spatial elements to test abilities relating to spatial imagination, spatial organisation, and spatial systematisation. The testee was given a drawing of a geometric figure and was asked to add it to a selection of simple shapes (a triangle, square, etc). This type of task consisted of simple volumetric elements that had to be combined to form a specific, three-dimensional entity.

In order to develop tests in this area, Ladovskii proposed that Krutikov use the mathematical theory of combination. Accordingly, Krutikov conducted some serious research, the results of which he included in a talk, given in the laboratory, and expounded in his article 'The Application of the Theory of Combination in Researching and Measuring Abilities for Spatial Combination' (dated 28 October 1927).

Krutikov regarded his research into an aptitude for spatial combination as a starting point for examining abilities relating to spatial composition. In this connection, within the framework of his investigation, he took the concept of 'spatial combination' to be 'the different possible arrangements of forms (planar and volumetric) as relating to one another in space (two-dimensional and three-dimensional)'. Using the method of mathematical analysis and the formulae of the theory of combination, the aim of the research was to 'elucidate the exhaustive possibilities for spatial combinations in general and within the limits established by us.' During the course of the study, it turned out that the formulae for the theory of combinations did not have the potential to establish the number of 'possible spatial combinations from these or any other flat or volumetric forms'. Therefore, using mathematical formulae, Krutikov developed new specific formulae for spatial combinations, which showed that spatial combination is a special instance of combination, because the formulae for the theory of combination did not take into consideration 'the possibilities for differently distributing one or another group of combinations in space.' Moreover, 'spatial combination also assumes the possibility of rotating a specific figure around its centre of gravity'.

'Generally speaking,' wrote Krutikov, 'spatial combinations can be limitless: you only have to move a figure at a slight angle to produce a new combination.' Nevertheless, when developing tests on the basis of the research that had been conducted, it was acknowledged to be less efficient to ask the testee to create a limitless number of combinations, than to find, within a fixed space of time, the greatest number of unique combinations, using, for example, two, three or four different geometric figures. As a rule, the tests consisted of two different pairs of forms. In order to ensure effective testing, Krutikov did not publish either the tests themselves or the investigative sheets (the possible rotation of simple figures, relating to a rectangular system of coordinates, and potential combinations of several pairs of forms).

A special 'individual category form' was developed to record the marks that were awarded during the various tests. On the basis of the complete set of tests, 'a psycho-technical profile of architectural skill' was established, which could then be used not only in selecting candidates for the Vkhutein's Architecture Faculty, but also by teachers in their further work with the students. Krutikov wrote:

Examples demonstrating the difference between the mathematical theory of combination and the theory of spatial combination.

Теория соединений	Теория простр. комбинирования		
$a, \quad b, \quad c$	□ ◸ ○ $a \quad b \quad c$	○ a ◿ b □ c	□ a ◿ b ○ c и т. д.

Теория соед.	Теория простр. комбинирования
a	□ a ◇ a и т. д.
b	b b b ◺ ▽ ◺ ◹ b ◿ b △ b и т. д.

Without yet knowing a student's work, but having his 'skills profile' to hand, the teacher was able, from the very beginning, to pinpoint those weaknesses that required attention. Later, in view of the fact that the skills levels did not remain constant, but usually improved in response to positive guidance, 'the profile' helped to chart the student's progress and make a completely objective and accurate assessment of the success of the architectural training.[13]

This was the first problem that Krutikov tackled within the framework of the psycho-technical laboratory, under Ladovskii's supervision.

THE INVESTIGATION OF MOVING FORMS
(THE ANALYTICAL COMPONENT OF KRUTIKOV'S PROJECT)

The second problem that Krutikov explored independently in the psycho-technical laboratory was that of mobile architecture (or moving forms). Krutikov was so fascinated by working on the problem of 'mobile architecture' that in practice he subordinated his diploma project to it, which then became, for him, almost an illustration of the solutions to the investigation that he had undertaken.

Krutikov's diploma project consisted of two parts – an analysis of the problem, and the design for a future city. The analytical component (the basic premises of the design) consisted of sixteen tables with illustrations (cuttings from magazines), plans, and a short explanatory text. In the first three tables, Krutikov considered the three basic problems of the 'theory of the architecture of moving forms'. Firstly, in table No. 1, he examined 'the visual distortion of moving forms'. Here, Krutikov defined:

> … two moments in the perception of moving forms:
> a) when the trajectory and the moving form are perceived separately…; and
> b) when the trajectory and the moving form combine to produce a new form and create a new entity with different qualities, both visually and physically.

This was followed by a description of the visual elements in the first table.

> 1. Lightning under 'the microscope of time' (at 1/100,000th of a second). The form of the lightning is visible.
> 2. The opposite phenomenon. The movement of an aeroplane on celluloid film.
> 3. The same in relation to the movement of the stars.
> 4. The effect of moving points of light (lights on a carousel in a Berlin park).
> 5 & 6. A car in different states (static and moving).

Secondly, in table No. 2, he looked at 'the composition of moving structures (in contrast to the composition of static structures)'. Here, Krutikov analysed the connection between static composition and verticality (the skyscraper), as well as the relationship between dynamic composition and horizontality (the airship, the steamship), introducing examples of contrasting combinations of stasis and dynamism ('flat railway lines with imagined train and semaphore signs'). He also tried to explain the principal differences between the composition of 'static structures' ('the intersection of compositional axes at a point, which is the destination of the movement: this point is found inside the building') and the composition of 'moving structures' ('a single extended compositional axis, directed towards the destination of the movement, which is located outside the building').

Thirdly, in table No. 3, he dealt with 'the generation of the form of the dynamic element'. Here Krutikov analysed the distinctive characteristics of the psychological perception of moving forms: 'two identical forms in movement are perceived as being of different sizes in relation to their position on the axis of the movement. The perceiver re-evaluates in his head the size of the forms in motion.'

In tables Nos. 4 and 5 of the analytical part of the project, Krutikov looked at the evolution of the shapes of motor cars, trains, ships, airships, and aeroplanes.

Table No. 6 was devoted to the problem of creating a unified 'means of water, ground and air transportation'. For Krutikov, this represented 'the aspiration to combine the possibilities of moving on the ground, over the water and through the air to create a universal apparatus in relation to the Earth's sphere'.

Table No. 7 contained examples of foreign mobile recreational vehicles, which Krutikov regarded as representing 'the seeds for mobile residences'.

A separate table, No. 8, was concerned with 'living conditions in contemporary mobile structures'. Krutikov indicated the level of comfort that could be devised for people staying in the interiors of various modes of transport, such as the deck of an airship representing a flying hotel, a cable car, an aeroplane-restaurant, a caravan, a children's room on a train, and the living quarters on a motor boat.

Table No. 9 analysed the conditions for 'the portability of moving structures', which Krutikov connected, above all, with the lightness of the material and the construction.

The following table, No. 10, demonstrated 'the aspiration of the technology of moving structures to reduce the space occupied by the machine and the general service areas in order to increase the amount of living space. Ideally, the machine should occupy no space at all'. Krutikov connected advances in this area with the evolution of energetics, the further progress of which he considered to be the fundamental factor that would enable the dreams of a mobile architecture to become reality. He wrote: 'Energetics stands on the threshold of a revolution, which must lead to the discovery of the possibility of using intra-atomic energy.' Reckoning on this energy, Krutikov designed his 'Flying City'.

Krutikov regarded the problem of a mobile architecture located above the Earth not only from the point of view of the technical possibilities, represented by various means of motion, but he also connected it with human skills and aspirations (tables Nos. 11-13). In Krutikov's opinion, buildings were evolving 'from the hut to the house in the air', reflecting 'humanity's aspiration to rise above the Earth'.

Krutikov devoted two tables, (Nos. 14-15), to examining the problems of 'conquering new spaces and new horizons'. In these, illustrations showed the Earth from above, the free air of space, a house in the air, the stratosphere, a rocket for inter-planetary travel, inter-planetary space, and cosmic space.

The analytical component of Krutikov's diploma project ended with table No. 16 in which contrasting juxtapositions showed how predictions and suggestions, which had been considered completely utopian or unacceptable not long ago, had now become a part of everyday reality. Krutikov presented an old caricature showing 'the horrors' of mechanical transport alongside an image of travelling in contemporary motor cars. He also presented different illustrations from the past which demonstrated the 'unprofitability' of the railways in comparison with horse-drawn transport (the engine was depicted as a monster consuming a mountain of cash), the unfeasible 'fantasy' of cable cars, and a ridiculous family outing in a carriage without a horse (a nineteenth-century cartoon), etc. This conclusion to the analytical portion of Krutikov's diploma project acted as a warning to the viewer not to make hasty judgements concerning the ultimate realism and future possibilities of realising his proposal, which comprised the design part of the diploma. He anticipated that it would be possible to share the fate of those 'dreamers' of the past, whose suggestions and proposals had now become actual reality.

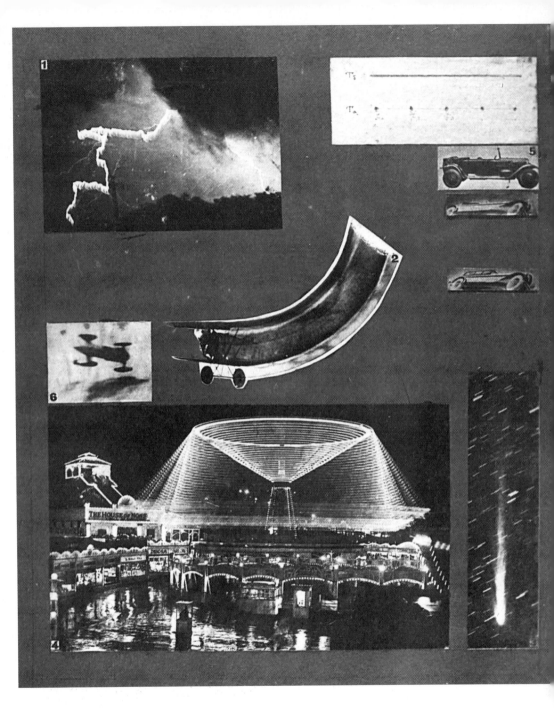

Table No. 1. The Visual Distortion of Moving Forms.

Table No. 2. The Composition
of Moving Structures.

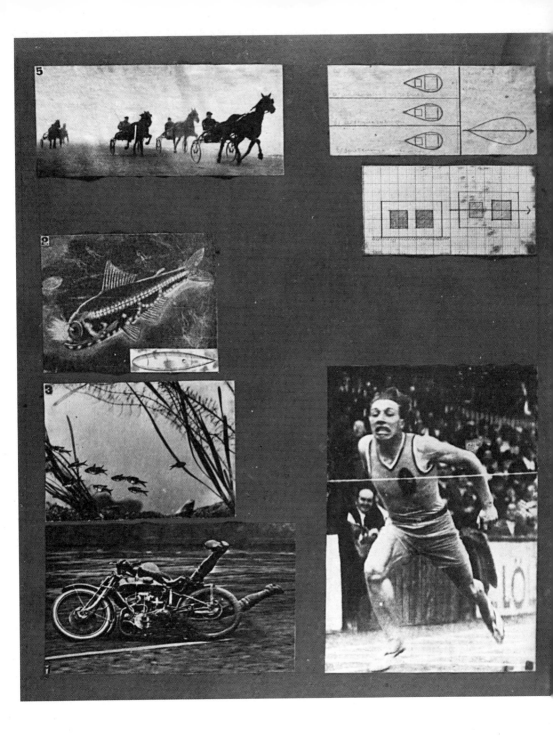

Table No. 3. The Formation of
the Dynamic Element.

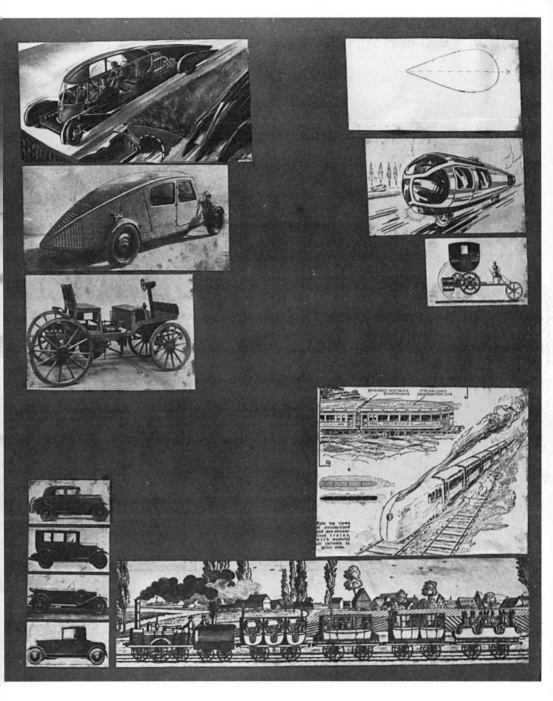

Table No. 4. The Evolution of the Forms of Cars and Railway Trains.

Table No. 5. The Evolution of
the Forms of Ships, Airships,
and Aeroplanes.

Table No. 6. Modes of Transport for Sea, Earth and Air.

Table No. 7. Rudimentary
Mobile Residences (Mobile
Country Homes in the West).

Table No. 8. Living Conditions in Contemporary Mobile Structures.

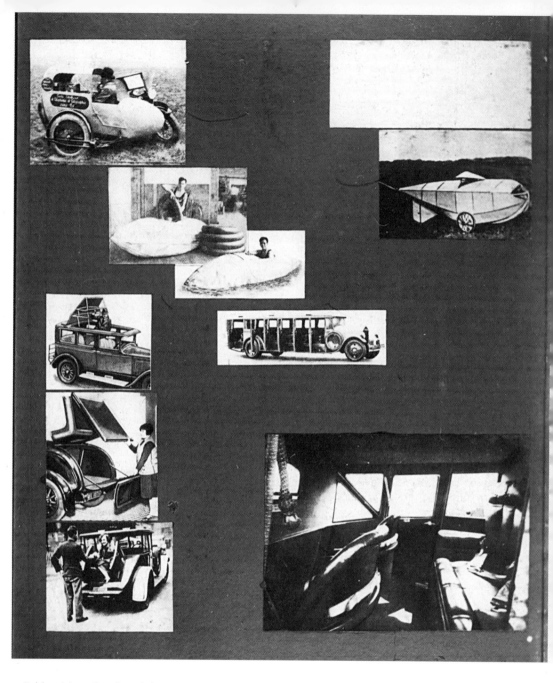

Table No. 9. Portability
of Mobile Structures (The
Lightness of Material and
Construction).

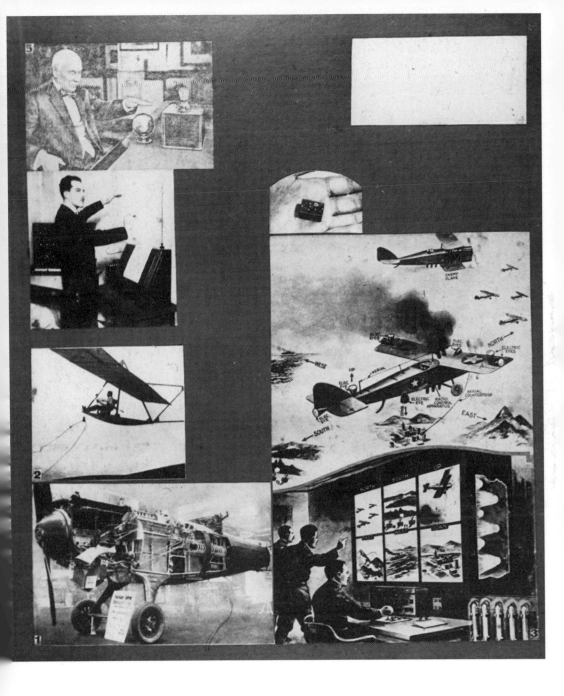

Table No. 10. The Evolution
of Energetics.

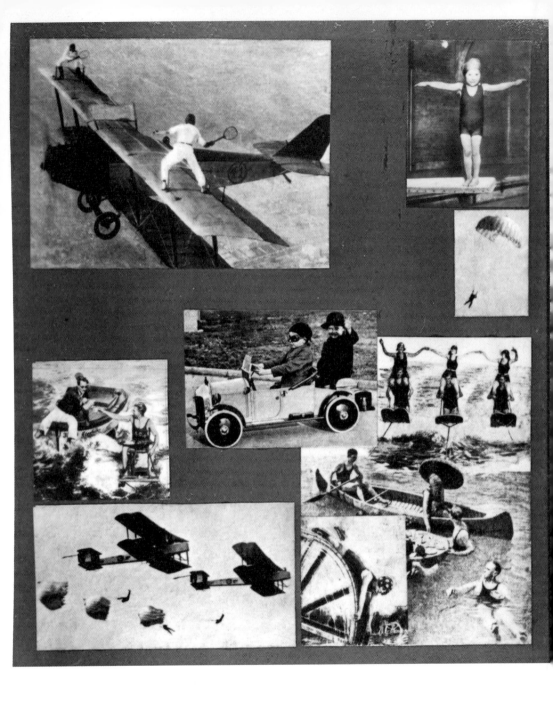

Table No. 11. Physical Culture
and the Future Man.

Table No. 12. The Evolution of Buildings (from Wooden Huts to Skyscrapers).

Table No. 13. Man's Aspiration to Extend his Horizons (Expanding his Perceptions of the Earth and the Universe).

Table No. 14. The Conquest of New Spaces and New Horizons.

Table No. 15. The Conquest
of New Spaces and New
Horizons.

Table No. 16. Dreams –
Fantasies – First Experiments
– Caricatures – Achievements.

DISCUSSIONS OF KRUTIKOV'S DIPLOMA PROJECT

To the credit of the Vkhutein, it is important to note that the examiners did not condemn Krutikov's project as an absolute fantasy. In general, the examination possessed a very distinctive character. The sensation and stir, which was evident in the Vkhutein's lobbies on the day of the project's examination, did not produce the enormous scandal that many had expected. Surprisingly, of all the examinations, Krutikov's was the 'quietest'.

It is possible that Anatolii Lunacharskii's article in *Izvestiya* about the diploma projects of the Vkhutein's Architecture Faculty had acted as a lightning conductor in deflecting criticism. Lunacharskii had visited the exhibition of the diploma projects in May 1928, a month before Krutikov's project had been completed and examined. What was important then was Lunacharskii's general judgement concerning the research work conducted at the Vkhutein in the area of town planning. The development of experimental diploma projects and visionary designs at that time helped to raise the general creative and theoretical level of the discussion of town-planning issues, helping them to be seen not only from the short-term point of view, but also from a long-term perspective.

This is how Lunacharskii evaluated the standpoints of these investigations:

In my opinion, the Architecture Faculty is the crown of the Vkhutemas. Here, there is an enormous range of practical, objective, accurate and graceful ideas, which can actually be related to our socialist construction. Young people often spread themselves too broadly. They are already dreaming of the town as it will be in 50 years time – but what dreams they have! – with unheard-of-until-now practical ideas, with the most accurate scientific data ... You leave the exhibition of the Vkhutein's Architecture Faculty positively refreshed, with an even stronger belief in our capacity for grandiose construction.[14]

But let us return to the examination of Krutikov's diploma project.

Krutikov was ill when he went into the exam. An electric atmosphere dominated the hall, which was full to overflowing. The tables of the analytical component of the diploma were on display along with the completed designs for 'The Flying City' effectively mounted on stretchers (some even like posters). Krutikov was very calm. Without any hint of pathos in his voice, he quietly and reasonably explained in detail the basic premises of his analytical work, the results of which had led him to place his 'future city' in the sky. Witnesses recall that a 'terrible quiet' reigned. Ivan Rylskii, the president of the examining committee, asked for questions. All the teachers and students at the Vkhutemas were silent. Only the representative of the city's department of communal economy on the committee (the architect Yakov Raikh) posed any questions. He asked, 'How much time have you spent on your diploma, how is all this to be sustained, and how will issues of sanitation and water supply be resolved in such a city?' Krutikov calmly replied that he had spent fifteen years thinking about the problem that was presented in his diploma project. In response to the second question, he answered that he considered that technological and scientific progress in the near future would undoubtedly allow this project to be realised. There were no further questions. Nobody spoke about the project. Rylskii hurriedly completed the examination process. Characterising Georgii Krutikov positively and mentioning his success during the course of his studies, Rylskii announced that he had been awarded the title of 'architect-artist'.

Scandal around the project of 'The Flying City' came later. Soon after Krutikov's diploma exam, a sharply critical article appeared in the newspaper *Building* (*Postroika*), written by the journalist N. Levochskii and entitled 'Soviet Jules Vernes: The Vkhutemas is not Training Builders, but Day-dreamers. The Construction Project "The Flying City"'. The article stated:

> What is our contemporary building industry required to do? To build good, comfortable, and cheap housing. Despite our most intensive efforts, we have not yet been able to achieve this. Nevertheless, at this time, the Vkhutemas, instead of training competent, business-like young specialists for the building industry, has been occupied with fantastic visions. Amongst the most glib, cheeky and stunning city designs is the project for a 'Flying City'...
>
> We have all enjoyed reading the novels of Jules Verne. And, in front of our eyes, the boldest of these novels has already become a reality.

Life, of course, outstrips the most fantastic dreams. But life must be constructed and developed according to the laws and inventions of technology, and not in accordance with the subjects of Jules Vernes's novels.

It is true that the novelists' visions of yesterday can become and do become the reality of tomorrow. It is possible to fantasise in novels. But if such a 'novelist' is allowed to build, then the result is not really a building, but a bad adventure novel ... with a criminal ending.[15]

Within a month, the same newspaper *Building* had published a response from the Presidium of the Architecture Faculty (comprising professors and students at the Vkhutein), entitled 'We are not Training "Soviet Jules Vernes": The Architecture Faculty is on the Correct Path'. The response stated:

Nobody is intending to build the future city today. At the examination, the project presented was not a 'Project for the Building of a Future City' but a 'Project for Resolving the Problem of the Future City'. Society has often expressed the desire that the 'diploma projects in establishments of higher education should be busy solving problems of a research nature'. In the Architecture Faculty, research problems are naturally concerned with the field of architecture. This includes, and must include, the subject of the 'future city'. We think that if only 5 students out of 100 produce their diploma projects as speculative formulations of a scientific research problem, this does not prove that the Faculty is removed from life.[16]

The rector of the Vkhutein, Pavel Novitskii also responded to the criticism of the diploma project in the newspaper *Building*. In reality, he was not only defending Krutikov's project but also trying to justify himself. Novitskii wrote that the author of the article in *Building:*

Had appreciated nothing ... had understood nothing, having glimpsed among 62 highly practical designs (completely valid both technically and artistically) one that dealt with the theme of 'The Flying City', he had immediately made a cheeky generalization concerning the visionary and utopian nature of the entire faculty. He knew that a significant proportion of the Architecture Faculty objected to 'The Flying City' project and regarded the architectural and theoretical value of this design to be utopian today, although architecturally justified.[17]

But criticism of Krutikov's project did not end here. During the next few years, 'The Flying City' was repeatedly mentioned, whenever it was deemed necessary to attack innovative design. The leaders of VOPRA (Vsesoyuznoe ob'edinenie proletarskikh arkhitektorov: All-Union Association of Proletarian Architects) were particularly zealous. In their battle against Leonidovism (*leonidovshchina*) and the architectural avant-garde in general, Krutikov's project for 'The Flying City' became yet another accusation that they could hurl at the Vkhutein for its 'training being remote from practicality'. Even in late 1930, one of the leaders of VOPRA, Arkadii Mordvinov, produced several articles and talks against Ivan Leonidov, which also mentioned the 'formalist' Krutikov.

In his article 'Leonidovism and its Evils', Mordvinov wrote of Krutikov's 'Flying City':

> The author based his design on the hypothesis that, through splitting the electron, a means will be found to easily raise a building into space, with cabins for residents. The Earth, freed from residential and community buildings, is to be for work and excursions. Communication with it is to be provided by means of a special capsule, which represents a combination of the motor car, the aeroplane and the submarine. After a trip under water, over the ground or through the air, it is possible to enter any hotel, also floating in space, in one of these free capsules ... Such projects were seriously examined at professorial meetings, and for this project, a diploma and title were awarded.[18]

GEORGII KRUTIKOV'S 'FLYING CITY'

I talked with numerous active and eminent members of the Soviet architectural avant-garde. Most of them, when discussing the most significant designs of the 1920s, mentioned Krutikov's 'Flying City'. The situation was somewhat confusing. My interlocutors asserted that Krutikov's project was never published. They remembered the framed drawings of Krutikov's design, and reproduced for me drawings of fragments of 'The Flying City', but for some reason, they were all convinced that Krutikov's diploma project had not survived, neither in the original nor in photographs.

At the same time, many of my interlocutors stated that Krutikov's diploma project was one of the most outstanding creations of Soviet avant-garde architecture. They said that the impression that Krutikov's 'Flying City' made could be compared with that produced by Ivan Leonidov's Lenin Institute. Vitalii Lavrov, who was Krutikov's friend and another one of Ladovskii's charioteers, informed me with complete confidence that Krutikov's 'Flying City' had disappeared. Apparently, he had prepared a second book on *The Architecture of the Vkhutemas* (the first was published in 1927), which was devoted to cities of the future. The visual material was all ready, and a special place had been assigned to Krutikov's diploma project. The publication, however, was shelved on the grounds that it was 'formalist', and all the prepared material was lost. Lavrov was convinced that in the circumstances of the battle against 'formalism', Krutikov's project could not survive.

I was not persuaded that the material of Krutikov's diploma had disappeared completely. But facts are facts – one of the most original designs of Soviet avant-garde architecture was only mentioned in a few articles, and both as a design and as an artistic phenomenon was completely absent from the history of Soviet and international architecture of the twentieth century. In continuing my search for Krutikov's designs for 'The Flying City', I paid particular attention to the private archives of his friends and fellow students at the Vkhutemas. At that time, students often exchanged photographs of course and diploma projects, and more than once this had helped me to shed light on the work of those avant-garde figures, whose own archives had not survived, but some of whose designs (photographs) remained in the archives of their friends.

Nevertheless, in relation to Krutikov's student works this general rule did not apply – there were no photographs of his designs in the archives of his friends, who vividly recalled his diploma project and were able to sketch parts of it. This situation continued until the end of the 1960s, when Vladimir Krinskii, one of the leaders of Rationalism, told me that Krutikov's daughter had some photographs and explanatory texts relating to the diploma project. I contacted the daughter, and through her met Krutikov's widow who still preserved the architect's extensive archive. This included the original analytical component of the diploma project, photographs of the design element of the diploma, and numerous typed and handwritten texts. I organised Krutikov's personal archive, which was subsequently given to the Shchusev Architectural Museum in Moscow, and in 1973 I published a long article 'The Design of the Flying City' in the journal *Decorative Art of the USSR* (*Dekorativnoe iskusstvo SSSR*). So, after 45 years, Krutikov's diploma project finally took its place among the masterpieces of Soviet avant-garde architecture.

The 1920s in Soviet architecture witnessed an extraordinary explosion of creative experimentation of such intensity that this period has almost no equal in the entire history of Russian twentieth-century architecture, nor perhaps in world architecture of the time. During these years, projects were created that not only seemed to totally reject tradition, but were also completely unrealistic. Innovative experiments destroyed the old conceptions and undermined the most well-established stereotypes. Many designs of these years exerted an enormous influence on the development of twentieth-century architecture, and were important creative innovations. Years have passed, and what seemed to be fantastic then, now seems completely feasible – *The Model for a Monument to the Third International* (Vladimir Tatlin); The Horizontal Skyscraper (El Lissitzky); The Lenin Institute (Ivan Leonidov); The Monument to Columbus (Konstantin Melnikov); The City on Springs (Anton Lavinskii), and many others. These and similar designs were repeatedly criticised in the 1920s and later for their speculative nature and lack of practicality. But at that time, all the supporters of the avant-garde saw them as the latest word in architecture and understood their role in the development of creative invention. This is evidenced by the fact that all these designs were repeatedly published in the specialist architectural press.

1. Feudalism and the period of transition to capitalism	2. Capitalism and the the period of transition to socialism	3. The future development of the city in socialist society

Plan | Elevation

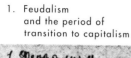

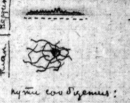

Means of transport:

The Horse | Automotive transport on the surface of the earth | Long distance and local air transport

THE ORGANISATION OF HOUSING

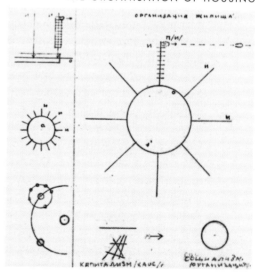

CAPITALISM (chaos)   SOCIALISM (organization)

Schemes Krutikov presented to illustrate some of the concepts of his diploma project.

Krutikov's project suffered a different fate. It is difficult to understand exactly what happened, but this very first design for a cosmic city in world architecture was not published at this time, although at the end of the 1920s in the Soviet Union there were numerous journals that were systematically publishing all the most interesting innovative designs. Apparently, the unusual nature of Krutikov's project and the originality of its striving towards the future exceeded even the very high level of appreciation for the role of creative experimentation that was characteristic of the 1920s and the avant-garde period.

Krutikov's project was not published during the years of the architectural avant-garde, nor during the period of the Stalinist Empire style, nor during the time of Nikita Khrushchev's utilitarianism. The years passed, and the time came for man to conquer the real universe, and in architectural circles people began to recall that there had been a shy but extraordinarily visionary student Krutikov, whose diploma project had caused a sensation at the time, although it did not seem to have surprised anyone at the Vkhutein. Both the project itself and the situation connected with its development and examination came increasingly to be surrounded by myth and rumour. As mentioned above, all of Krutikov's friends, including those who had helped him in the final stages of drawing the project's design, believed that it had been lost. But fortunately, the design had survived, and was published (after a delay of 45 years), and it came to occupy its rightful place among the masterpieces of Soviet avant-garde architecture.

We will now examine the design component of Krutikov's diploma project, widely known among architects as 'The Flying City' although Krutikov himself always called his diploma project 'The City of the Future (The Evolution of Architectural Principles in Town Planning and Residential Organisation)'. He considered that within the evolution of human settlements, his project represented a specific stage in man's mastery of the Earth and space.

According to Krutikov, 'The City of the Future' was to consist of two basic elements: 'the vertical – the residential component; and the horizontal, on the surface of the Earth – the industrial component'. Both the element on the ground (the industrial) and the element above the Earth (the residential) were, in principle, static i.e. stationary, and situated in specified areas of the Earth's sphere. In this respect, the title 'The Flying City' does not reflect the fundamental idea of the spatial organisation of Krutikov's 'City of the Future'.

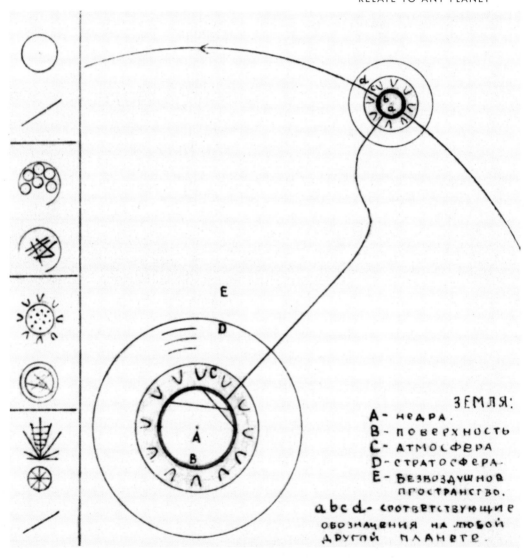

THE EARTH:

A - THE CORE
B - THE SURFACE
C - THE ATMOSPHERE
D - THE STRATOSPHERE
E - AIRLESS SPACE

abcd - ARE FEATURES THAT
RELATE TO ANY PLANET

ЗЕМЛЯ:

A - НЕДРА.
B - ПОВЕРХНОСТЬ
C - АТМОСФЕРА
D - СТРАТОСФЕРА.
E - БЕЗВОЗДУШНОЕ
ПРОСТРАНСТВО.
abcd - СООТВЕТСТВУЮЩИЕ
ОБОЗНАЧЕНИЯ НА ЛЮБОЙ
ДРУГОЙ ПЛАНЕТЕ.

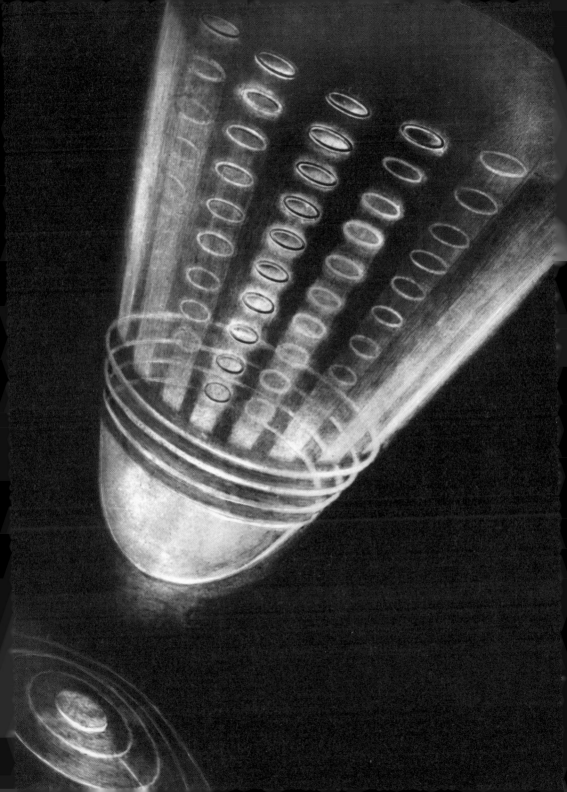

The city itself did not fly; the residential elements were freely 'suspended' in space, but were inseparably connected with their fundamental city-forming element – the industrial component, which was situated on the Earth.

Krutikov oriented the spatial structure of 'The City of the Future' around the paths of communication through the air. Consequently, it was not the city that was 'flying', but its inhabitants. The earthbound industrial component had a centric spiral ground plan. From its developed centre, the industrial territory extended outwards, expanding towards the periphery and curving in a spiral. The residential quarters of the city were suspended above the industrial territory in the form of an upside-down paraboloid, on a vertical axis that was oriented towards the centre of the earthbound part of the city. The envisaged exterior of the paraboloid, with its many storey, soaring in space, was to accommodate residential complexes. Krutikov proposed a spatial organisation for the transport paths through the air that linked the residential quarters with the workplace – the basic 'main road' went along the axis of the paraboloid, from which other 'roads' branched off. In the living quarters – radial roads (the tiers were piled one on top of the other) led to the separate residences, and in the industrial part – radial spiral roads led along the axes to specific industrial areas. Krutikov considered that technology's rapid progress would produce a revolution in transportation. In his opinion, the development of mass air transport (for short and long distances), and particularly the emergence of a universal means of individual travel, which also possessed the comfort necessary for short stays (the mobile living capsule – which was autonomous, but also an integral part of the static residential structure), would permit the Earth to become free from transportation structures and allow residential and public buildings to be located in space.

Communication between the Earth and the soaring buildings in space was to be effected by means of the universal travel capsule (the cabin), which could move through the air, along the ground, through water and under water. Krutikov regarded this cabin as a mobile living capsule (for short stays), providing human beings with the necessary comforts when travelling and living beyond the limits of 'The Flying City'. The capsule-cabin was equipped with self-cleaning walls and collapsible, multi-functional furniture for one person. Krutikov thought that the very shell of the capsule should be elastic. Depending on the position of the person (sitting, lying, etc), the shell could easily change shape and adopt one that would be convenient for the occupant, without losing its fundamental structure.

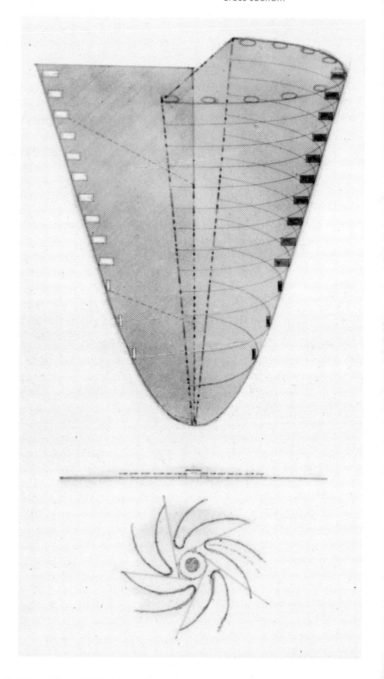

'The Flying City'. Plan and cross-section.

THE MOBILE COMPONENT OF THE RESIDENTIAL STRUCTURE

Work room

Room for relaxation

Social space

THE INTERNATIONAL NATURE OF THE MOBILE CAPSULE

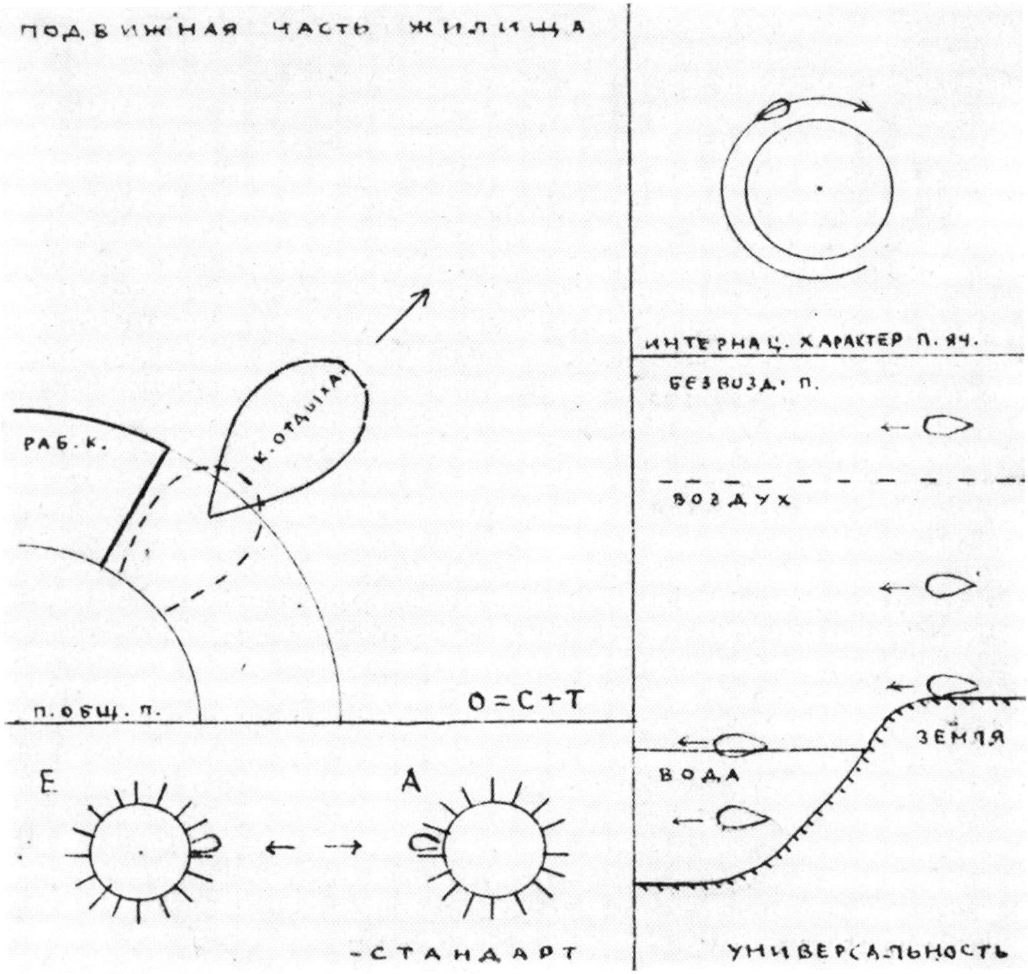

ПОДВИЖНАЯ ЧАСТЬ ЖИЛИЩА
РАБ. К.
К. ОТДЫХА
П. ОБЩ. П.
О=С+Т
Е
А
СТАНДАРТ
ИНТЕРНАЦ. ХАРАКТЕР П. ЯЧ.
БЕЗВОЗД. П.
ВОЗДУХ
ЗЕМЛЯ
ВОДА
УНИВЕРСАЛЬНОСТЬ

Airless space

Air

Earth

Water

STANDARDISATION

UNIVERSALITY

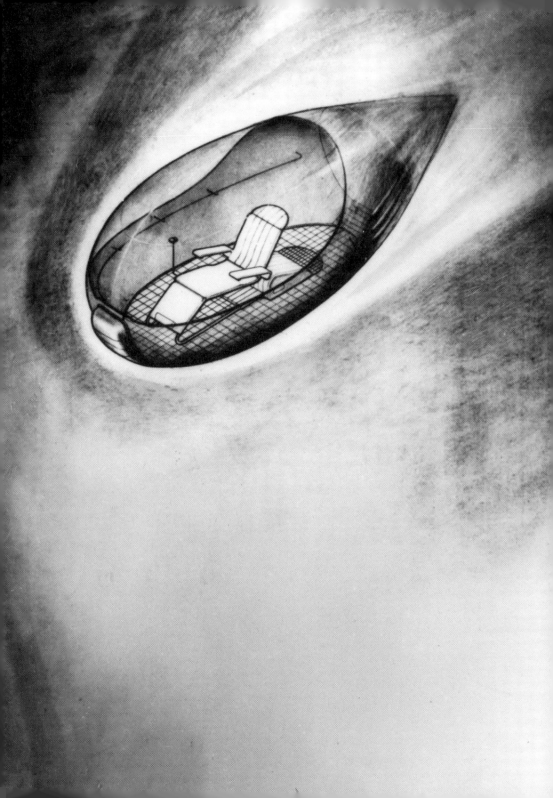

p. 76: The Cabin, the universal means of transportation for 'The Flying City'.

First type of living quarters developed for 'The Flying City'. Cross-section and general view.

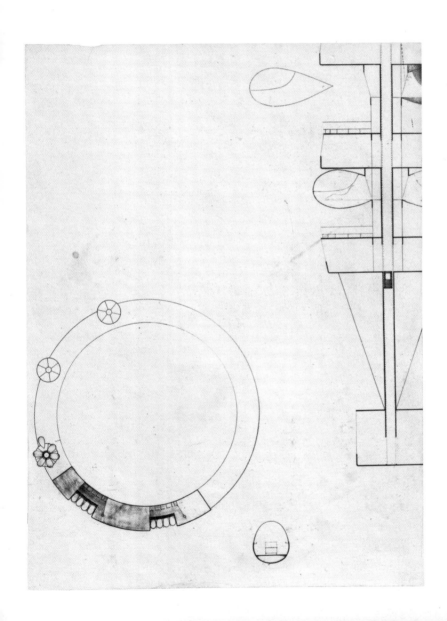

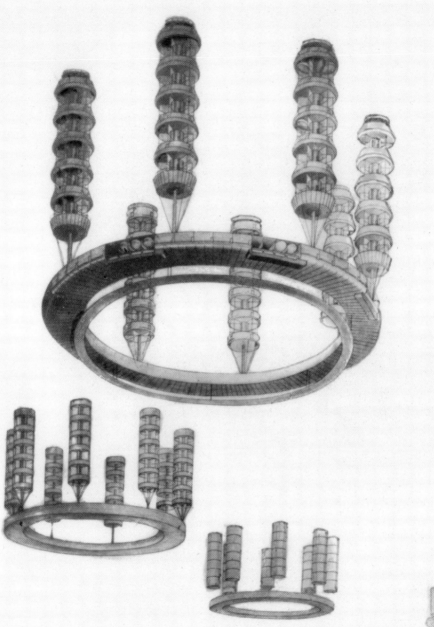

Second type of living quarters developed for 'The Flying City'. Cross-section and general view.

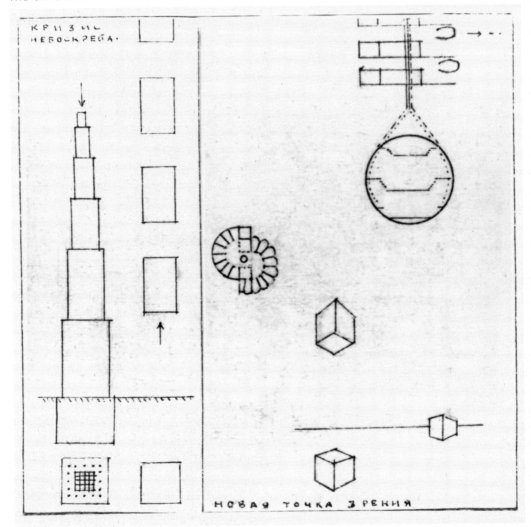

КРИЗИС НЕБОСКРЕБА.

НОВАЯ ТОЧКА ЗРЕНИЯ

Third type of residential structure for 'The Flying City': the Hotel. Façade and cross-section.

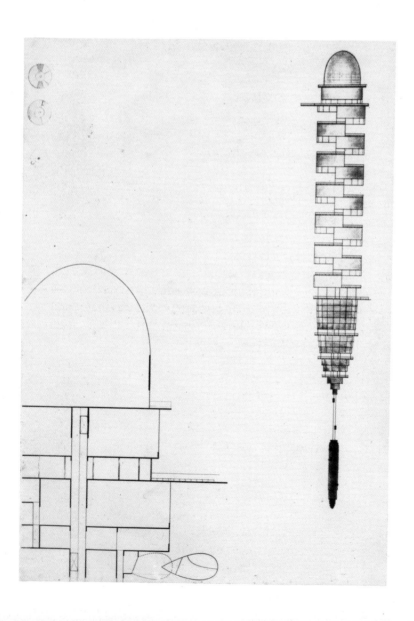

The cabin could be guided without a control lever – by movement of the hands, intersecting with strong lines of electromagnetic field. The mobile living capsule could easily fit into the buildings, which soared in the air, and Krutikov considered it to be a mobile and autonomous component of the static building.

The static living quarters were designed as three basic types.

The first type was the working commune, which represented a complex ensemble, consisting of eight vertical, five-storey living structures, joined together by lift shafts with a horizontal ring-shaped communal building positioned below: 'a vertical structure containing premises for individual use joined to a communal ring'. Each storey of the circular residential building was divided into six individual living capsules. Each living capsule consisted of a high loggia, the upper portion of which provided an arrangement for the final approach and mooring of the mobile capsule-cabin. The living quarters were located above this. All three elements of the individual living accommodation (the loggia, the mooring for the mobile cabin, and the basic living space) were connected with each other vertically and with the lift shaft. The ring-shaped communal structure contained rooms for various purposes as well as a honeycomb of loggias where mobile capsule-cabins could be moored for brief stays.

The second type of housing, according to Krutikov's text, 'is the result of the concentration of the spatial components of the first variant: all the verticals are collected into one large cylindrical form, a ring is assembled into a sphere, and the same with the premises for public use'. The eight-storey residential building was joined to the spherical communal building by means of a lift shaft.

The third type of housing was the residential 'hotel', which was apparently located outside the boundaries of 'The Flying City', and was intended for temporary residents and short stays. This vertical building consisted of three different components with separate functions and structures: the lower part was a multi-storey system of 'honeycombs' for the temporary mooring of mobile capsule-cabins; the middle structure was similar in its organisation to the residential building of the second type; and the upper section was a building for public use.

These types of 'static residences', which were suspended in the sky, formed 'The Flying City' or, more accurately, those sections of Krutikov's complexly structured 'City of the Future' that were suspended above the Earth.

ПОДВИЖНАЯ /ЭЛАСТИЧНАЯ/ ПЛАНИРОВКА.

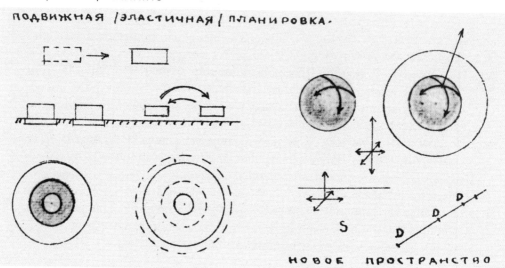

НОВОЕ ПРОСТРАНСТВО

A NEW SPACE

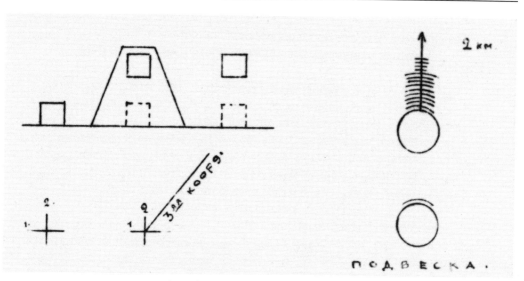

ПОДВЕСКА.

The 3rd coordinate

SUSPENSION

The design and spatial structure of Krutikov's 'City of the Future' was intended to provide a convenient link between the residential and industrial components and to provide the potential for their future development. Nevertheless, Krutikov did not allow technology to play a decisive role in determining the specific form of the 'City of the Future'. Instead he gave priority to social and architectural problems. This is evident from the structure and content of his 'Theses' for the diploma project which are cited below in full:

ARCHITECT G. T. KRUTIKOV

Theses for the Project 'The City of the Future'
(The Evolution of Architectural Principles in Town Planning and Residential Organisation)

The fight for the architecture of the future is the fight of today.

I. THE SOCIAL ASPECTS

The international nature of the mobile capsule. Expanding horizons. The disappearance of the state. Communist society.

A higher level of spatial organisation, corresponding to a higher level of social organisation.

Instead of linear chaos on the chaotic surface of the Earth there is a graceful organisation in the freedom of three-dimensional space. Linear chaos and the perfection of the circle as spatial contrasts, corresponding respectively to: firstly – the anarchistic and individualistic world of capitalism and secondly to socialism.

Nevertheless, the system of spatial perfection and co-ordination allows the possibility for future free growth and development, conducted in the areas of planetary organisation, the creation of distinct social settlements, the organisation of residential buildings (workers' communes), and separate housing for individuals.

The rational economic organisation of the Earth's sphere and the rational use of the Earth's space.

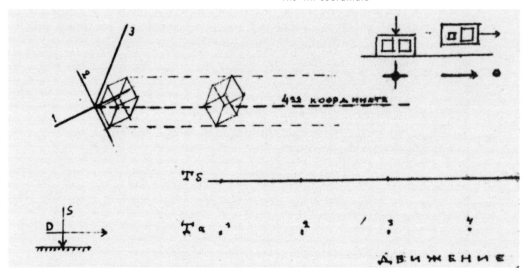

МОVEMENT

EXPANDING THE HORIZON: A) SPATIAL B) CEREBRAL

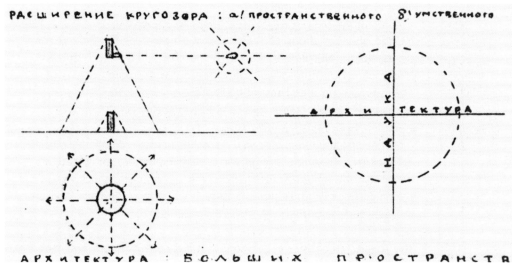

Architecture | Science

THE ARCHITECTURE OF VAST SPACES

The principle of **flexible planning** (planning that can adjust to changes in the way that the living social organism inhabits the city).

The expansion of the architect's outlook beyond the limits of a narrow class context. The broad connection between architectural questions and all problems stimulating scientific thought.

II. THE ARCHITECTURAL ASPECTS

The introduction of the **dynamic** element into architecture, the fourth co-ordinate of space (time). The particular perception of moving form. The architecture of mobile structures. The architectural expression of moving form.

The use in town planning of the third co-ordinate of space (height). The architectural expression of suspended forms. The expansion of architectural horizons in connection with suspending forms high in the air and introducing a mobile element. (The principle of housing with expanded outlooks). New points of view.

The architecture of large spaces. Architecture on Earth and in three-dimensional space. Its advantages.

The nature of general expression in the new architecture.

III. THE TECHNICAL ASPECTS

The universal nature of the capsule in respect of moving in various media (water, earth, air). Contemporary technological research to combine these movements (water, earth, air).

On the path of the revolution in energetics (intra-atomic energy). The jet engine.

Contemporary technological sources for the mobile capsule of suspended architecture (the development of the weekend caravan, the suspended cable car, the airship-sanatorium, the helicopter, the gyropter, etc).

In their turn, new architectural and spatial solutions present technology with new problems.

The first practical steps: an aspiration to lightweight residences (lightweight materials and construction). The introduction of mobile aspects in housing and the implementation of flexible town planning in accordance with the contemporary state of technology.

1 JUNE 1928 MOSCOW

Despite the project's superficial fantasy, Krutikov himself considered that it would be a fully realisable proposition in the not too distant future. He carefully followed all the innovations in the field of science and technology that related to the problems he was tackling. The list of books and journals in Krutikov's bibliography for the 'City of the Future' is revealing. The first section dealt with the 'Social Sciences'. The second section was 'Space in Nature', which included books on astronomy (Arthur Eddington, *Stars and Atoms* of 1926; Harry Schmidt, *Relativity and the Universe* of 1922; and others), the natural sciences (Vladimir Vernadskii, *The Biosphere* of 1926; George Clarke Simpson *New Ideas in Meterology*, 1923 etc), and mathematics (Albert Einstein, *Relativity: The Special and General Theory* of 1920; Nikolai Lobachevskii, *Pangeometry* of 1855, etc). The third section, 'The Technology of Transport', consisted of works relating to ground, water and air transportation (Konstantin Tsiolkovskii, *Air Transport*, of 1916, and Vladimir Obraztsov, *The Encyclopedia of Communications* of 1925, etc), as well as aeronautics (Tsiolkovskii, *The Exploration of Cosmic Space by Means of Reaction Devices* of 1903; and Nikolai Rynin, *Interplanetary Communications* of 1928-1932, etc). In addition, there was a long list of specialist journals in English, French and German, dealing with issues of rail, road, air and water transport, as well as aeronautics. A special section of the bibliography included books and journals on architecture and town planning.

Krutikov studied the problems of air travel and aeronautics with particular intensity. He was especially interested in the potentials of the airship and jet engines. As mentioned above, in the 1920s the future of air transport was mainly connected with airships. At this time, Krutikov not only closely followed all the innovations in the field of airship construction, but also, in the mid 1920s, began to experiment with airship design himself.

88

In connection with this mode of transport, he paid particular attention to the gondola or passenger cabin. Krutikov's drawings for these designs reveal his aspiration to approach the gondola as an initial prototype for a dwelling, suspended above the Earth: its volumetric and spatial structure, its plan and outward appearance, and its relatively large size, which permitted the creation of those comforts that were essential for a human sojourn inside.

The airships built by Ferdinand von Zeppelin enjoyed the greatest popularity in the first third of the twentieth century (a strong system with a metallic skeleton, covered in fabric). These airships were used in military action during the First World War and were then employed for carrying post and passengers across the Atlantic. Built in 1928, the airship 'Graf Zeppelin' was shown in Moscow (1930) and completed a series of long flights.

The last passenger airship built according to the 'Zeppelin system' was 'the Hindenburg', which was built in 1936, and made 63 flights, but was destroyed by fire in 1937. With this disaster, the era of the airship came to an end. But this was later – in the 1920s the production of airships increased rapidly, their structure was improved, and new construction systems were developed: soft, semi-hard and hard. Construction systems were also developed on the basis of the design proposed by Tsiolkovskii in 1887 for an all-metal airship without a carcase, which could change its volume while in flight. Krutikov knew of Tsiolkovskii's design and based his own work on this project. He turned for advice to Tsiolkovskii and wrote him several letters, which have perhaps been preserved in Tsiolkovskii's archive.

THE PROBLEMS OF FLEXIBLE TOWN PLANNING

After having defended his diploma project, Georgii Krutikov continued to be preoccupied with the problems of 'flexible planning', but he approached this problem broadly, without producing a specific proposal like 'The Flying City'. Krutikov understood perfectly well that the creation of a form of housing 'suspended' in space only had relevance as an essentially speculative idea, at least in the short term. At this time, however, the problem of flexible or adaptable planning was already of real and practical importance: Nikolai Ladovskii was actively working in this area.

In the first few years after graduating, Krutikov expanded his sphere of interests as an architect, designer and researcher. He wrote in his autobiography: 'After graduating, from 1928 to 1933 I worked as an architect in the Moscow Building Trust (on housing construction), the State Institute of Urban Design (on town planning) and the People's Commissariat for Enlightenment (on building theatres).'

In April 1929, Krutikov gave a talk to the planning section of the State Institute of Construction in Moscow on the subject of 'The Principle of Flexible Planning'. The theses of this talk are as follows:

ARCHITECT G. T. KRUTIKOV

The Principle of Flexible Planning (Theses of the talk given to the planning section of the State Institute of Construction)

1. The city as a living organism.
2. The inadequacies of predictions.
3. The need for continuous adjustments to the spatial organisation of the city over time.
4. The means of resolving this problem in the conditions of the anarchistic and individualistic organisation of capitalist society:
    a) Reconstructive surgery.
    b) Temporary building.

5. The spatial possibilities of planning in the conditions of Soviet construction.
6. THE PRINCIPLE OF FLEXIBLE PLANNING.
7. The creation of FLEXIBLE 'planning material' in relation to development.
8. The development of ORGANISATIONAL and transformative types (industrial, technical and spatial possibilities).
9. Fundamental questions concerning the spatial organisation of cities (growth, size, form, etc) from the point of view of the new principle.

APRIL 1929
MOSCOW

In his paper, Krutikov talked about a flexible spatial and planning structure, which would allow the city to change quantitatively and qualitatively in response to corresponding changes in life itself.

The second document preserved in Krutikov's archive that deals with the problem of flexible planning is also dated April 1929 and, judging by its content and organisation, is connected with the first document. Here it is in full:

Schematic Programme of Work for the Planning Sub-Committee

I. THE PROBLEM OF THE CITY
Settlements of urban types; their categories; reasons for the emergence, growth and decline of towns. General analysis. Social and Economic factors:

1. Types of towns, their size according to population and area.
2. Systems of town planning, ideal cities. Satellite towns. Specialist towns.
3. The principles of creating urban districts according to function, and zoning in accordance with development.
4. The elements of a town.
5. Static and dynamic town plans.
6. Transport problems in planning a town: the road network, trams, railway junctions, airports, etc.
7. The problem of industry and urban construction.
8. City defences and the urban population.

II. DEVELOPMENT

1. The choice of location for planning and its proposed requirements.
2. Types of planning for residential areas and districts. Building zones. Regulations.
3. The system of districts and internal development for large, medium and small-scale construction.
4. Changes in the forms of urban areas caused by increased building.
5. The process of expanding and improving city buildings, and systems for replacing one type of building with another.
6. The forms of planning for industrial areas and their relationship to residential districts.
7. The nature of districts for public buildings: administrative, cultural and educational, etc.
8. The system of green areas. Types and norms.
9. Systems of buildings for physical culture. Types and norms.

III. THE PROVISION OF PUBLIC AMMENITIES

1. The connection between planning, development and various systems for providing public amenities.
2. Systems for providing public services, in relation to towns of various sizes, purposes and characters.
3. Sanitation networks and technical arrangements – their impact on the town, their location.
4. The sanitary and technical equipment for a cluster of developments.
5. Protection against wind, and adaptation to climatic conditions, air flow in the town.

IV. THE WORKING METHOD

Collecting material. European and Russian examples. Their examination and analysis. Conclusions and proposals. Checking with existing plans.

V. STAFF

Permanent employees: *the problem* – 2 people; *development* – 2 people; of these, one is the secretary. Papers on particular problems: each month – 2.

GK
12 APRIL 1929

In 1930, Krutikov was still working on the problems of the new town. In his archive there is a document dated December 1930, entitled 'The Architectonics of the City'. I will present it in full:

The Architectonics of the City

The architectural appearance of the socialist city and the contemporary Soviet city during the period of reconstruction and the transition to socialism.

1. The principles of spatial organisation for socialist and capitalist cities.
2. The social and class expression of urban architectonics.
3. Elements and principles of urban architectonics in an historical context.
4. The architectonics of the contemporary Soviet city:
   a) Planned anew.
   b) In the context of the rationalisation and reconstruction of the legacy of the past.
5. The architectonically specific characteristics of the towns of the Soviet Union in relation to their local, social way of life, geophysical and climatic particularities, and also in relation to the town's political importance.
6. The practice of urban architectonics in the Soviet Union and abroad.

7 DECEMBER 1930
ARCHITECT G. KRUTIKOV (SIGNATURE)

Demonstration stand for the
design of the Town-Commune
'Avtostroi' at the Soviet section
of the *International Exhibition
of Decorative Arts* in Milan
(Italy). 1930.

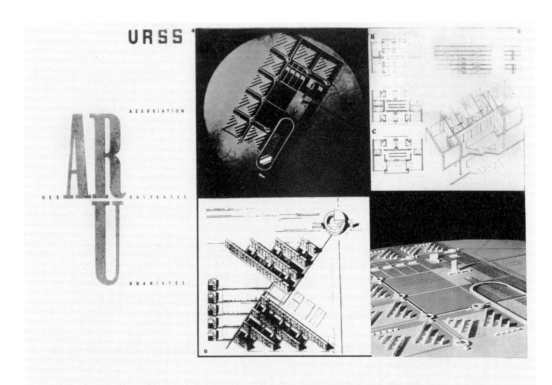

THE TOWN-COMMUNE 'AVTOSTROI'

Krutikov's competition design for the town-commune 'Avtostroi' (*Avtomobilnyi stroitel'stvo*: 'Automobile Construction') corresponded perfectly to his work on the problems of the new town.

At the end of the 1920s and beginning of the 1930s, when creative organisations had already been consolidated, the most important projects were implemented through invited competitions. Designs were commissioned directly from creative organisations: MAO (Moskovskoe arkhitekturnoe obshchestvo: Moscow Architectural Society); ASNOVA (Assotsiatsiya novykh arkhitektorov: Association of New Architects); OSA (Ob'edinenie sovremennykh arkhitektorov: Association of Contemporary Architects); ARU (Ob'edinenie arkhitektorov-urbanistov: Association of Architects and Urbanists); and VOPRA (Vsesoyuznoe ob'edinenie proletarskikh arkhitektorov: All-Union Association of Proletarian Architects). The members of these groups themselves determined who would participate in the competitions. Collective designs were created by brigades or teams.

The competition for the project of planning and building 'Avtostroi' (a town based around the Nizhny-Novgorod car factory) was announced in 1930 as a competition by invitation. ARU's participating team consisted of Georgii Krutikov, Vitalii Lavrov and Valentin Popov.

The competition brief, developed by the clients, stated that it was intended to create a town-commune for 50,000 inhabitants, initially for 25,000 (of whom 14,000 would be workers). A green zone was to be provided between the factory and the housing districts. In the brief, all the arrangements relating to the social and domestic aspects of the life of the inhabitants of the town-commune were set out in detail:

...

4. In planning the workers' settlement, it is vital to take into account the fact that this settlement must be a town-commune, in connection with which, the following factors must be taken into account in the planning:

   a) Services for the younger generation are to be conducted communally by providing a full coverage of nurseries, homes, nursery schools, and boarding schools ...

   b) Feeding the population will be centralised by means of the organisation of food factories, capable of servicing the entire population, and the food produced will be distributed through cafeterias and cafés in the House of Culture and in the park ... premises for consuming food at the factory ... and cafeterias and cafés in the communal houses ... In the cafeterias and cafés of the communal houses, the products of the food factory will be provided as fully prepared or semi-ready meals.

   c) Cultural work by means of the construction of a House of Culture and the provision of spaces in the communal houses for travelling libraries, rooms for relaxation, a cinema, a radio installation, a place for physical exercise, study rooms, etc.

   d) Physical culture by means of organising a centre in the House of Culture, and subsidiaries in the communal houses.

   e) Sanitary services through the construction of:
      1) A bath-house with showers and bathing facilities
      2) Showers in the communal houses, and
      3) Laundries.

5. The Residential buildings:

   a) Communal housing to be built for 24,000 people.

   b) ... for a single inhabitant ... the living-space norm must be no less than 7 square metres ...

   c) In the communal houses, attention must be paid to the following:
      1) Every room must be equipped with running water.
      2) The cafeteria and cafés must have facilities for preparing and heating food received from the food factories (cafeteria capacity should be 200 people per 1,000 inhabitants of the communal house).
      3) A travelling library with a reading room.
      4) A room for meetings and a room for relaxation with a radio installation.

> 5) Study rooms.
> 6) A retail and information centre i.e.
>> a) Shop for the sale of paper, stamps, small domestic items and haberdashery, fruit juices, biscuits, cold snacks, rolls, preserves, etc.
>> b) A post office, a telegraph, a savings bank, an information office, and a newsagents' kiosk.
> 7) Showers, bathrooms, toilets, and a utility room …
> 8) A hairdressers …
> 6. … Residences comprising individual flats are to be built for 300-500 families.[19]

The design by the ARU team developed the competition brief further. The authors minutely examined each item of the social provisions and the reconstruction of everyday life (the planning of the residential blocks of housing as two variants – sleeping capsules for one or two people or individual two and three-roomed flats). The Residential district was divided into eight sections – residential complexes of two components, each for 2,940 people. Each section was adjacent to the park area, which abutted the city centre and the school district. Each living complex comprised six-storey residential buildings with crèches in between them. The nurseries and the circular community building (with cafeteria, auditoria, libraries, a gym, etc) were situated on the edge of the sections. All the buildings in a section were joined by heated passages.

The evidence suggests that in designing the town-commune 'Avtostroi,' Krutikov was not only a co-designer, but also the theoretician. Two versions of the explanatory texts for this project have survived, both of which were signed by Krutikov alone. One of these, the abbreviated version, is preserved in Krutikov's archive. These three type-written sheets, dated 17 April 1930, were produced especially for an exhibition in Milan where the project for the town-commune 'Avtostroi' was shown, accompanied by a short variant of the text in Italian. The longer version of the text was published in the journal *Soviet Architecture* (*Sovetskaya arkhitektura*, No. 2, 1931).

I consider it essential to publish the short version of the text almost in full (with a few omissions) because the versions can be read in different ways, and this variant clarifies some formulations of Krutikov's ideas about town planning:

ARCHITECTS: KRUTIKOV, LAVROV, AND POPOV.

The Town-Commune 'Avtostroi' (for 50,000 inhabitants, attached to the factory built near Nizhny Novgorod).

The planned construction of the USSR's economy and the rapid tempo of the country's industrialisation has raised various issues concerning the new organisation of workers' settlements, which are emerging just now in relation to provisions for those who are in the process of building (constructing) the industrial giants of the Soviet Union (Magnitostroi, Stalingradstroi, Kuznetskstroi, Zaporozhe, Avtostroi, etc).

These settlements, emerging in the country that is building socialism, must be towns of a socialist type, possessing all the characteristics of the socialist economy and way of life.

In the case of the present project for the town-commune 'Avtostroi', we are trying to establish the distinctive features for the organisation of a socialist settlement – those special characteristics that have already received graphic architectural expression.

In terms of space (in relation to spatial solutions), the socialist town is not considered as a mechanical combination of areas, but as a unified, elegantly organised, industrial and residential complex. To give the clearest **architectural and spatial expression** to this specific organisational entity is the fundamental task of the current planning solution.

This expression is attained by:

1. The unified logical and rational arrangement of the component elements of the urban complex, with an emphasis on the communal aspect and on arrangements that will increase the potential for social contact towards the public centre of the entire settlement (the House of Culture);
2. Contrasting spatial and textural characteristics of the basic elements of the urban complex (the assembled and relatively dense constructions of the residential areas, and, in contrast, the park-like solution for the communal areas, etc) ...

ARU Team (Georgii Krutikov, Vitalii Lavrov and Valentin Popov), Town-Commune 'Avto-stroi'. Competition design. Plans, cross-sections and axonometric projection of the residential block: variant for the communal housing — sleeping modules; variant for the individual apartments, and plans for the social block. Model of the Town-Commune. 1930.

АВТОСТРОЙ - 3

II. THE RESOLUTION OF THE TOWN PLAN

The centre of the urban complex is the communal area ... located in a park, adjacent to the River Oka. This community element – the park – acts as the organising and unifying centre for the public life of the town. On three sides (on the left) it is surrounded by residential areas, on the fourth side (on the right) it abuts the industrial district – the motor car factory ... with the technical college ... and the food factory...

The social life of the town already possesses a graceful organisation through the territorial distribution of its constituent elements.

In the residential (quiet) zone, protected as much as possible from through-traffic, we have provided space for **individual** relaxation and group (team) interaction. Additionally, the communal complexes (in the form of a ring) located at the edges of the zone, afford possibilities for extensive **collective** social contact. Finally there is the centre for mass culture, comprising the House of Culture, the whole park, and, developing towards the river, a system of squares, avenues, places for physical culture, a sports stadium, a motor track, and a water-sports centre – all this taken together provides a springboard for **mass** events (demonstrations, community festivals, physical contests, etc).

Side by side with this grand centre facing the river, the communal element of the town possesses another centre with buildings of an administrative and economic function, located towards the factory.

In this area, we have the Central Outpatients Hospital, the bath-house, the laundry, the fire station, the centre for the allocation of goods and the distribution network, an hotel for visitors, and finally, at the crossroads where these two axes meet, the town's Soviet. The hospital is located on the edge of the settlement.

The town's domestic traffic travels along enclosed highways, which encircle the perimeter of the factory and the communal areas of the town.

This inner highway is joined to the inter-city highway (between Nizhny-Novgorod and Dzerzhinsk), which links the town with the surrounding motorways.

III. THE HOUSING SOLUTION

The residential district is organised into building complexes of two types:
1) **Sleeping residences** (elongated, narrow buildings).
2) **Communal residences** (in a ring shape).

The sleeping residential complexes meet the needs for individual relaxation, mainly sleep, and consist of smallish rooms (of about 7 square meters each), which are like rationally equipped cabins with folding furniture, a washbasin and shower. These rooms, assembled on a floor (without a corridor) and isolated from all noise, are interspersed with floors that have a communal function ... the purpose of these floors is to bring the most vital and elementary services (a snack bar, halls for morning exercise, rooms for individual and group study, verandas and a winter garden), as close as possible to those who are relaxing.

The communal residential complexes (ring-shaped) are places for social contact of an already significantly collective nature; it is estimated that each residence will be able to serve up to six thousand people a day.

Each residence contains a collection of subsidiaries of the Central Institution of Services for the entire settlement.

There is a branch of the House of Culture, with a large hall for general meetings of the residents' group. This also functions as a lecture hall and a cinema (Central Sector). In addition there is a group of rooms for academic study, with a mobile library attached; a branch of the food factory – a circular cafeteria; a first-aid point (a branch of the Central Outpatients Hospital); a shop (an outlet of the central network for the distribution of goods); a fully equipped gym with an adjacent area for sports, including a small stadium, a running track, and a sports ground; and finally a garage with motor cars for communal use.

The Children's Section of the town-commune has its own specific system of structures (nurseries, nursery schools, etc), which are not, however, separated into a special children's village, but are closely linked with the life of the adults.

Hence the nurseries (for babies and children 0 to 3 years old) are linked to the adults' sleeping and living complexes by means of heated passageways. Although the nursery schools (for children 3 to 7 years old) are not linked with the adult residences by means of heated passageways, they are close to them (... the buildings, which are square in plan, are grouped to the left).

Only the schools with their specific domestic arrangements and noisy life are separated into a special school village, which is, however, situated in the immediate vicinity of the residential district...

Attention is drawn to the dynamic nature of the design for the residential arrangements, in the sense that they possess the potential to gradually adapt to different degrees of a communal way of life, which would entail only an insignificant alteration in the organisation of the buildings' internal partitions.

In this way, without making any special buildings for families or preserving an individual domestic economy and isolated family way of life, there is the potential for two and three-roomed flats, located in the same buildings, which, with a slight refitting, can be adapted to institute a communal way of life and the economic organisation of a town-commune.

... the two lower plans ... show the arrangement of two and three-roomed flats, and the upper plan ... the distribution of individual cubicles in the same building.

In the axonometric drawing, it is possible to see the internal furnishings of the individual cabins.

17 APRIL 1930
MOSCOW
ARCH. G. KRUTIKOV

ARU Team (Georgii Krutikov, Vitalii Lavrov and Valentin Popov), Town-Commune 'Avto-stroi'. Competition design.

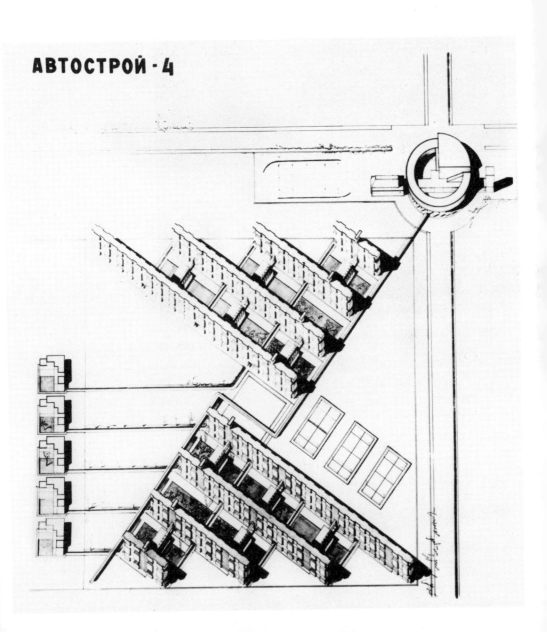

АВТОСТРОЙ · 4

PERFECTING THE COSMIC THEME:
THE MONUMENT TO COLUMBUS

In 1929, Georgii Krutikov, together with Andrei Bunin and Trifon Varentsov, participated in the International Competition for a Memorial Lighthouse to Christopher Columbus at Santo Domingo, Dominican Republic. All the competitors received a plan of the area and a short brief, which specified that:

> Given 2,500 acres of waterside property for what is to become a carefully restricted Pan-American Park; the problem first of all is to find the best site for the Columbus Memorial Lighthouse ...
>
> The reservation to be developed embraces the location of the original city that Bartholomew, the brother of Christopher Columbus founded. Also on it stands the ruins of the Dominican Church of the Rosary, the oldest Christian church in the Western Hemisphere ...
>
> In this work of planning for the stately development of a vast tract of land and of designing a great monument, the competitor is confronted with no ordinary problem ...
>
> The competitor is, therefore, to design a monument which shall exercise a power over the mind that the current architecture of the day, with all of its obvious perfections, does not possess ... What is desired then is something that is fresh and new, spirit and substance, as well as form, a noble monument with a message, which shall contribute something to knowledge and thought.[20]

The collective competition entry clearly reflected Krutikov's 'cosmic' passions. The monument consisted of two spheres – a large one below, symbolising the Earth, and a smaller sphere, which was lit up and raised high up on a mast, denoting another planet. The mast was faced with mirrors and, when viewed against the sky, it either disappeared or 'was lit up' by the sun's rays, recalling the trail of a rocket, moving away from the Earth towards another planet.

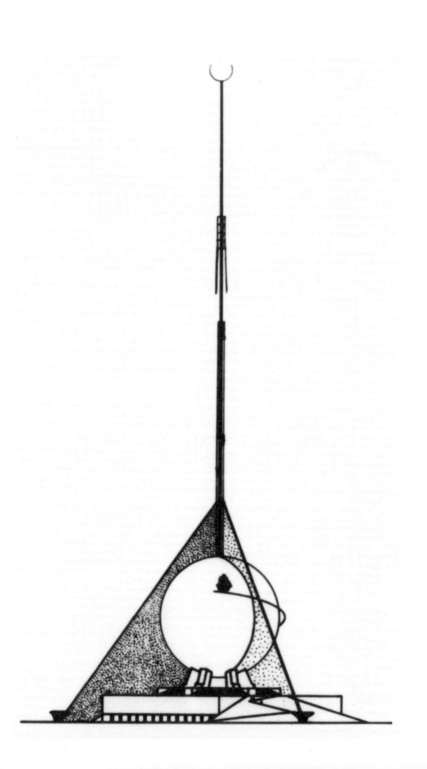

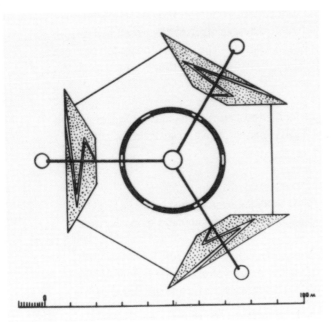

Andrei Bunin, Trifon Varentsov and Georgii Krutikov. Design for the Memorial Lighthouse to Columbus at Santo Domingo. International Competition. General view (p.104), façade and plans.1929.

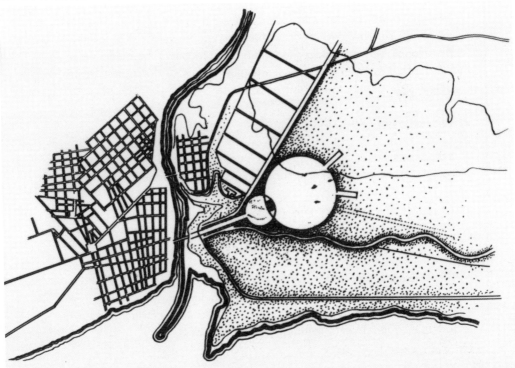

The imaginative solution for the monument reflected the designers' ideas – Columbus had initiated the epoch of great geographical discoveries (a sailing boat moves around the large sphere in a spiral – the ship of the epoch of great geographical discoveries) – while ahead lies the path to other worlds, the epoch of discovering the Universe.

An explanatory note to the project, comprising five pages of typescript, is preserved in Krutikov's archive. I am reprinting an extract from this text.

1. The Idea

The fundamental core of the monument's message – is humanity's victory over nature and its space, and the **gradual extension of humanity's spatial horizons**.

Beginning with the insignificant movement over **the surface** of the Earth, humanity is now about to cover the entire **volume** of the Earth's sphere and is on the threshold of discovering vast new **spaces**, beyond the confines of the Earth.

The epoch that began with Columbus – the epoch of exploring the Earth – has ended; we are now standing on the verge of **great new discoveries**, beyond established limits. And recalling the **bold step** of the intrepid traveller of oceans, we must get ready for a **new, even bolder step** – the leap into universal space.

2. The Means of Expression

It is constructed in accordance with the stated idea, and the **architectural composition** is based on the inter-relationship of two spherical forms …

The spiral line which envelopes the Earth's sphere and along which Columbus's ship is travelling, concentrates the viewer's attention on the historical event to which the monument is dedicated.

The monument's pedestal, which principally extends as flat and horizontal elements, articulates various stages in the early development of human culture and provides a logical approach to the further elaboration of the fundamental meaning of the monument.

This element of the structure mainly employs the resources of a planar layout and sculpture.

In contrast with the entire Pan-American Park, which has the physical appearance of untouched nature, this pedestal area must bear the imprint of a strict organisation imposed on nature by man's hand. It includes a layout of grand squares, flowerbeds, fountains, etc.

At the base of the pedestal is a large gallery and loggia with internal staircases leading to a terrace …

The central portion of the monument, symbolising, as already stated, the Earth's sphere, is a ceremonial building for Columbus's tomb, which is to be transferred from the cathedral …

Columbus's medieval tomb, just like his caravel (ship) already mentioned, is taken into account architecturally, and presents a sharp contrast to the contemporary architecture – the architecture of new ideas, new materials, new technical possibilities and new forms.

EXHIBITION DESIGN

While he was still a student, Krutikov had been involved in the artistic design of two exhibitions: *The All-Union Polygraphic Exhibition* in Moscow of 1927, for which he designed the stand for the journal *The Spark (Ogonek)* ; and the Soviet pavilion at the *International Pressa Exhibition* in Cologne in 1928, where he was responsible for 'The Lenin Corner' and the spatial construction 'The Structure of the USSR'. Both of these shows were created under the direction of El Lissitzky, who by the end of the 1920s had become the acknowledged leader in developing new approaches to exhibition design. His ideas were effectively demonstrated at these exhibitions and others of 1927-1930, which were created by artistic collectives under his direction.

The *All-Union Polygraphic Exhibition* was Krutikov's professional introduction to the new concepts of exhibition design and it took place in the main hall that had been built for the *Agricultural Exhibition* of 1923. The existing interior did not please Lissitzky, so he and his collective radically transformed it to create a new display area. The open frameworks were encased in smooth coverings, and the forms of the ceiling were hidden by a decorative honeycomb of hangings. This almost weightless ceiling then became a widely used device in exhibition design. For the show itself, several different types of simple constructed stands were developed, built up from standard components.

For Krutikov, the *Polygraphic Exhibition* marked an important stage in his mastery of the professional methods of exhibition design. Even before this, in 1926, he had been in creative contact with Lissitzky. Together they had explored the architectural problems of airship construction. Now, under Lissitzky's supervision, he assimilated the methods of designing an exhibition space. Krutikov was a very talented pupil and in the following exhibition (*Pressa*, Cologne 1928), he worked virtually as Lissitzky's equal.

The Soviet Section at the *International Pressa Exhibition* was an important event in the development of exhibition design. One of the artists who worked on it, Vladimir Roskin, recalled:

> When we did this exhibition, it created a sensation like an exploding bomb. No other country in the whole world had yet developed such a way of showing propaganda material ... The theme of the exhibition was displayed in figurative constructions – types of three-dimensional posters ... Some stands were conceived as original three-dimensional diagrams.[21]

These stands were created by individual artists like Nikolai Prusakov, Mikhail Plaksin, Grigorii Borisov, Grigorii Miller, Aleksandr Naumov, Sergei Senkin, and others. Yet, for some reason the publications did not mention specific authors in relation to several of the three-dimensional stands. It has been assumed that Lissitzky himself made these, although as artistic director he had distributed the stands amongst the members of the artistic collective, while retaining overall control. Among the installations not attributed to specific designers are two of the most striking in terms of artistic skill: 'The Lenin Corner' and the central installation – 'The Three-Dimensional Star'. Careful study of Krutikov's archive has allowed us to eliminate this gap in creative authorship.

In one of his undated autobiographical texts, Krutikov wrote: 'Even before graduating, I executed some works for the building of the International Red Stadium on the Lenin Hills [today the Sparrow Hills] Moscow in 1924-1926; and for the *All-Union Polygraphic Exhibition*, held in the Central Park of Culture and Rest in 1927. In 1928, "The Lenin Corner" and the central installation – "The Structure of the USSR", for the Soviet pavilion at the *International Pressa Exhibition* in Cologne, were executed according to my designs.'

Krutikov's authorship of 'The Lenin Corner' is confirmed by two design drawings in pencil: a façade and an axonometric projection with its dimensions. The façade is signed by Krutikov with the date: 28 March 1928. Comparison of these drawings with the stand 'The Lenin Corner' executed at the exhibition allows no doubt of Krutikov's authorship. This means that this stand should be described as: 'Georgii Krutikov, Three-dimensional stand "The Lenin Corner"' at the *International Pressa Exhibition* in Cologne (supervisor El Lissitzky).

There are also no grounds at all for doubting that Krutikov also designed the central installation, which used the construction of a three-dimensional star. Krutikov's archive contains a photograph of this installation, from the German magazine *Der Welt-Spiegel*, 3 June 1928, and a photograph of 'The Three-Dimensional Star', which may also have been built for the exhibition *Children of the Soviet Union*.

Krutikov, Three-Dimensional Stand 'The Lenin Corner' for the *International Pressa Exhibition* in Cologne (supervisor El Lissitzky). Axonometric projection (p.110), elevation and photograph.1928.

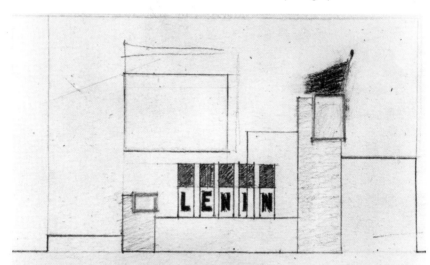

M. 1:100   28/ⅩⅡ 28.

The construction of the three-dimensional star (preparatory model of the exhibition stand).

Krutikov, Central Stand (The Three-Dimensional Star) at the *International Pressa Exhibition* in Cologne (designer-in-chief El Lissitzky). 1928.

p. 117: Display of aeronautics at the Rally of Young Pioneers and the exhibition *Children of the Soviet Union* in Moscow in 1929 (aeroplane and airship).

Krutikov's success in exhibition design did not go unnoticed, and in 1929 he was appointed the chief architect (working at the head of a large collective) for the exhibition *Children of the Soviet Union*, to take place on the land previously used for the *Agricultural Exhibition* of 1923.

The exhibition *Children of the Soviet Union* was timed to coincide with the opening in Moscow of the All-Union Pioneers' Rally. The rally and the exhibition included various elements in the open air for the participation of the pioneers, coming from all over the country, as well as the opportunity to view displays in the exhibition's interior, including the presentation of the contemporary achievements of science and technology, such as aeroplanes and airships. Once again Krutikov was in his element – he had actually suggested including aeronautical items in the show. Even so, Krutikov's main focus in this exhibition (in collaboration with Sergei Senkin) was on creating the interior spaces. Krutikov did not repeat what Lissitzky had done with this very same interior in 1927 for the *Polygraphic Exhibition*. He did not decorate the open construction of the interior, but made that construction part of the general exhibition space, exploiting various significant features of the architecture. In some of the volumetric and spatial stands, Krutikov even reinforced the constructive essence of the new architecture.

The pioneers' rally took place in autumn 1929. In spring of that year, the Central Park of Culture and Rest had opened in the very same place, i.e. where the *Agricultural Exhibition* had formerly been held. For that reason, much of the work of organising the area for both the park and the rally took place simultaneously. This had a particular impact on the small architectural structures. For the park, Krutikov designed a kiosk for Mosselprom (Moskovskoe ob'edinenie predpriyatii po pererabotke produktov sel'skokhozyaistvennoi promyshlennosti: The Moscow Association of Enterprises Processing Agricultural and Industrial Products), which was intended to sell all types of retail products. This kiosk was the first architectural design by Krutikov to be actually built.

At the end of the 1920s and beginning of the 1930s, Krutikov actively participated in a whole series of competitions, as a member of the team from ARU. These included the House of Culture for the Proletarskii District of Moscow, the Monument to Columbus, the Town-Commune 'Avtostroi', the Theatre in Sverdlovsk, the Palace of the Soviets in Moscow, and others.

Installation for the exhibition
at the First All Union Rally of
Young Pioneers in Moscow.
Views of the interior. 1929.

p. 121: Kiosk for Mosselprom,
for all types of retail items in
the Central Park of Culture and
Rest in Moscow. 1929.

If we add his course project for a Higher Art College and his diploma project 'The Flying City' to this list, we could say that Krutikov's avant-garde period of creative work, which included three student designs and five collective competition entries, lasted a mere 5-6 years. The majority of these works have been examined above. Let us consider the rest.

The ARU Team (Georgii Krutikov, Vitalii Lavrov, Sergei Lopatin, Valentin Popov). Competition design (first stage) for the Palace of Culture of the Proletarskii District in Moscow. Plan and model. 1930.

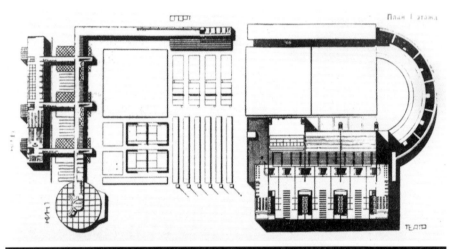

TACKLING THE ARCHITECTURAL PROBLEM OF THE NEW THEATRE

At the beginning of the 1930s, theatres were considered to be some of the most important public buildings and were attracting a lot of attention. There were competitions for designing theatres in large cities, like Kharkov, Rostov-on-Don, Sverdlovsk, Moscow, Ivanovo-Voznesensk, and Novosibirsk. Moreover, the theatre was regarded as a major urban building with a universal function, which seems to have derived from the Houses of Culture: it was a place for mass spectacles, different forms of which were being actively developed at this time by innovative directors, particularly Vsevolod Meyerkhold.

During this period, Krutikov was interested in the problem of designing a theatre building to perform a universal role. In 1931-1933, he was the academic secretary in the architectural office responsible for building theatres within Narkompros (the People's Commissariat for Enlightenment). As part of a team, he developed competition entries for a Palace of Culture in Moscow (which included a theatre) and for theatres in Sverdlovsk and Moscow. He also wrote analytical articles, participated in discussions and prepared a collection of articles about the problems involved in the architectural design of theatres.

Krutikov's archive contains unpublished manuscripts: articles, minutes of meetings, and a plan for a collection of articles. The contents of these manuscripts, which are dated 1931-1932, complement the articles about the issues of theatre architecture that Krutikov published in the early 1930s, in the journals *The Building Industry* (*Stroitel'naya promyshlennost'*), *Soviet Architecture* (*Sovetskaya arkhitektura*), and *Architecture of the USSR* (*Arkhitektura SSSR*).

I am reprinting some fragments from these three manuscripts.

The ARU Team (Georgii Krutikov and Sergei Lopatin) and ASNOVA (Mikhail Korzhev). Competition design (second stage) for the Palace of Culture of the Proletarskii District in Moscow. Plan and model. 1930.

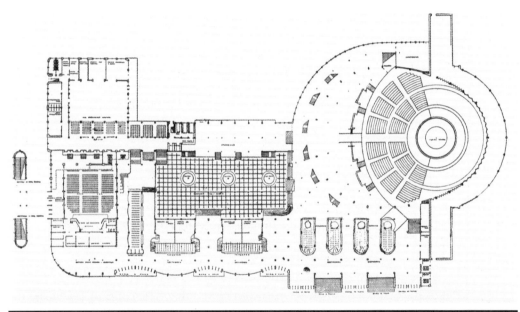

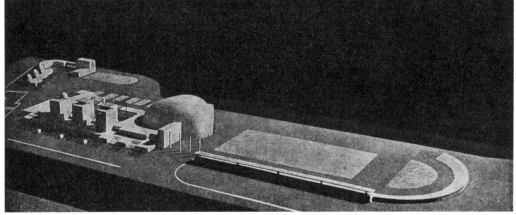

The first manuscript:

G. KRUTIKOV

The Construction of Theatre Buildings

… The significant increase in the number of new municipal theatres under construction during the period 1933-1937 (115 theatres in the Russian Federation alone) demonstrates the seriousness of the current task. At the present time, the absence of sufficiently convincing and adequately developed types of theatre buildings … calls for more well-designed, scientifically researched and experimental work. Today, in design, we have three basic trends in the organisation of the theatre as a visual entity: firstly there is the theatre with a deep stage; the second is the theatre that has abandoned the deep stage for a stage in space (placing the stage in the middle of the auditorium or producing actions that surround the spectators); and thirdly, the theatre that combines a deep stage with one in the round. As a rule, theatres being built at the present time tend to be organised like the traditional type of theatres that everyone knows, with a deep stage …

At the present time, the construction of theatres of the latter two types is still at an experimental phase, and it is necessary to test these theatres in practice. In the arrangement of their spaces and in their architectural expression, all the theatres being built should convey the cultural and educational nature of the Soviet theatre which focuses on the masses. Therefore, in the foyer, space should be provided for cultural work with the audience during the intervals (exhibitions, workshops, etc). Provision should also be made for the possibility of using the theatre building for conducting mass meetings, congresses, and revolutionary festivals.

The second manuscript:

The Architectural Office for Theatre Construction within Narkompros

Minutes of the meeting of stage workers concerning questions of 'organising the stage and activating the auditorium', 26 February 1932 …

Chairman: Comrade Dedyukhin (member of the Narkompros Collegium). Presentation by the architect Krutikov concerning ways of organising the stage and activating the auditorium.

Discussion

Comrade Kurilko mentioned the positive aspects of the **standardised qualities of the old theatres**... The performance area in the form of an arena or stadium raises enormous difficulties in terms of set decoration, theatrical costumes, etc, because these are all presented against the chance backdrop of the spectators sitting opposite... The reform of the stage must be conducted on the basis of the latest technical achievements ...

Comrade Tairov considers that the question of activating the auditorium in the ways that have been suggested in contemporary architectural design is incorrect ...

We do not need to activate the auditorium, but to activate ideas ...

The theatre is an art of direct communication, of one person to another. The theatre is an art about people, but people have been forgotten and even the actor has been forgotten. It is impossible to consider only the mechanical aspects of activation ...

Tairov mentions the exceptional desirability of uniting the stage with the area for mass activities ...

It is essential to endeavour to develop elements of light and colour ...

Comrade Novitskii considers that it is vital to answer the question: what form of participation should the mass spectator take in the action?

The theatre itself must subordinate all technological possibilities to its theatrical aims ...

Comrade Dedyukhin dwells on the issue of the division between the architect and the theatrical workers. In this respect, the Art Department of Narkompros is at fault, because up until now it has only considered the problem of artistic form. The differences between the architect and the actor have not facilitated progress in this direction ...

Also the issue of the form of the 'connection between the actor and the spectator' has not been resolved ...

Architect Bogdanov considers that it is important to ask the question who has fallen behind – the architect or the director?

A representative from the Institute of Experimental Psychology announces that 'the excessive jolt to the spectator's expectations, which is present in some of the designs, is completely wrong from a psychological point of view.

The third manuscript:

The Architectural Office for Theatre Construction (Narkompros RSFSR)

Plan for a book concerning the design and building of theatres.
To mark the 15th anniversary of October.

Publication by the Architectural Office for Theatre Construction within Narkompros. Stroisnab, 1932.

General editor and author of the introductory article A. V. Lunacharskii.

A few general articles on the specific problems of theatre construction:

1. Architect Krutikov. Theatre architecture. Issues of designing and building (1929-1932) in the Soviet Union. Concerns relating to the use of the historical cultural legacy and the achievements of contemporary theatre building abroad.
2. Professor Lifshits. Acoustics for the theatre auditorium.
3. Questions relating to the organisation and mechanisation of the stage. Foreign advances in contemporary technology for the theatre. Issues concerning the standardisation of the stage.

Private and competition projects (1929-1932):

1) The Theatre for the Proletarskii District of Moscow 1929-1930
2) Rostov-on-Don, 1931
3) Novosibirsk, 1931
4) Kharkov, 1931
5) Ivanovo-Voznesensk, 1931
6) Sverdlovsk, 1931
7) The Theatre for the MOSPS Moscow, 1931-1932
8) The Meyerkhold Theatre, Moscow, 1931-1932
9) Smolensk, 1931

Text: 2 typed sheets.

Illustrations 40 pages, 100 photographs on coated paper. An artistic publication on good quality paper, well illustrated. Title page, table of contents, notes, and captions to the illustrations, in three European languages. Format ...

23 JUNE 1932
ARCHITECT KRUTIKOV (SIGNATURE).

As can be seen from these documents, Narkompros's Architectural Office for Theatre Construction was one of those scientific research centres dealing with the architecture of community buildings that was working effectively at this time. And Krutikov played a major role in researching the problems of the spatial organisation of the new theatre. He analysed competition designs in the press, and also, as one of Ladovskii's charioteers, developed competition projects. Moreover, Krutikov did not separate out the design of the theatre building from the rest of the project in the competition for the Palace of Culture for the Proletarskii District of Moscow, but considered the organisation of the cultural centre and the new theatre as a single problem.

Krutikov's first attempt at writing on this subject was the article about the competition designs for the Palace of Culture for the Proletarskii District of Moscow, published in 1930. In this text, Krutikov dotted the i's and crossed the t's in relation to the fundamental creative, scientific and experimental problems of the new theatre. He wrote:

Basically, the designers had to present solutions to the following two issues:

1) **The theatre**, i.e. above all, the architectural and spatial solution for the complex of 'the auditorium-stage', taking into account the work of contemporary theatrical collectives as well as the possibility of the future development of theatrical culture in the context of the new social structure.

2) **The cultural complex** – the completely new architectural and spatial complex for the community, intended to serve the cultural needs of a large working-class district.

Krutikov went on to analyse both problems, paying particular attention to the demands of the new theatre.

The new theatre needs:

1) The spatial potential for unifying the large collective of the audience through the spectacle alone;

2) To take into consideration the substantial growth of this collective, and, consequently, the possibility that the 'auditorium' and 'the stage' could be expanded;

3) To erradicate the division between the auditorium and the stage, and also use of all possible spatial aspects for activating the auditorium;

4) To make it possible for the intense dynamism of contemporary life to penetrate into the theatrical action.

Krutikov also explained some of the solutions to the problems of the new theatre proposed in the competition design by the team from ARU comprising himself, Vitalii Lavrov, Sergei Lopatin and Valentin Popov – Ladovskii's charioteers. Krutikov wrote:

The Principles of ARU. The chain of the ring of rows is disrupted, while the axis of the auditorium is turned through 90° and is placed parallel to the stage; providing the potential for a substantial expansion of the auditorium, without significantly increasing the distance from the stage – even for the back row. The extended front of the stage (served by a conveyer platform) permits the possibility of displaying and developing considerable dynamism ...

ARU. Plan of the Area. The Theatre. Facing the square for activities and connected with the stadium, it possesses a significant number of entrances.[22]

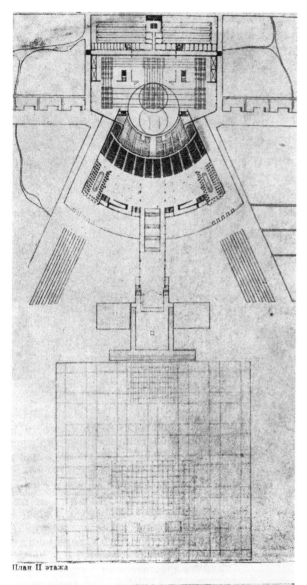

План II этажа

азрез

The ARU Team (Krutikov, Lavrov, and Popov). Competition design for the Great Synthetic Theatre in Sverdlovsk. Plan, cross-section, model and façade. 1931.

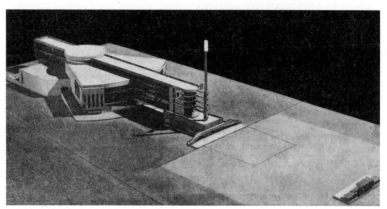

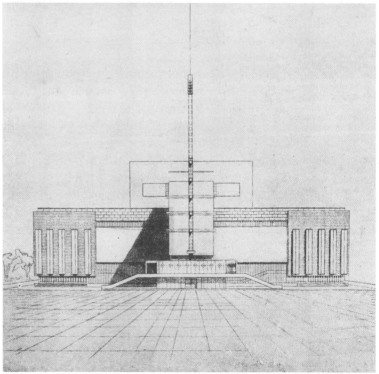

For the second phase of the competition for The Palace of Culture of the Proletarskii District of Moscow, the Rationalists entered as a single team, combining ARU (Georgii Krutikov and Sergei Lopatin) and ASNOVA (Mikhail Korzhev). Once again, Krutikov wrote an article analysing the designs of this phase of the competition.

In 1931, the ARU team (Krutikov, Vitalii Lavrov and Valentin Popov) entered the competition for designing the Great Synthetic Theatre in Sverdlovsk. Again Krutikov published an analysis of the competition.

The competition entries were judged by the delegates to the XVII Congress of the Communist Party, and official recommendations were produced for developing the final design. These recommendations in effect suspended re-search into the volumetric and spatial articulation of a theatre for mass action.

Among the competition designs for the theatre in Sverdlovsk, there were many original solutions towards developing an adaptable hall, and new archi-tectural visions (the entries from ASNOVA, as well as those of Ilya Golosov, and Moisei Ginzburg). These projects by eminent architects did not overshadow the ARU design, the creative concept of which was distinguished by its unusual volumetric and spatial composition.

In fact, designs by figures associated with the architectural avant-garde essentially retained their avant-garde appearance until the end of 1932, when they became influenced by the official results of the second phase of the Palace of the Soviets competition. These results initiated a process of stylistic change in Soviet architecture – a tendency to assimilate the traditions of the classical orders emerged and became increasingly powerful. During the phase of Post-Constructivism (1932-1936), Soviet architecture rapidly embraced the Stalinist Empire style. The creative problems of the new theatre were abandoned.

During the 1930s, Krutikov's design work underwent the same stylistic changes as that of other Soviet architects. For this reason, within Krutikov's creative oeuvre, only work executed before the end of 1932 can be related to genuinely avant-garde ideas and to his texts on the problems of the new theatre. These include his competition entries for the Palace of the Culture for the Pro-letarskii District of Moscow and for the Great Synthetic Theatre in Sverdlovsk.

The two variants for his competition design for the Vladimir Nemirovich-Danchenko Musical Theatre in Moscow (with Valentin Popov) are already in a purely and highly artistic Post-Constructivist idiom. The content of Krutikov's articles on the problems of theatre architecture also changed. Proposals for reconstructing the theatre became increasingly less prominent. In this respect, Krutikov's article 'The Design and Construction of Theatres in the USSR' (1934) is revealing. In this, he even explained and justified his earlier radical suggestions for the reform of theatre architecture. This was unusual self-criticism by an avant-garde figure. This is what he wrote:

In recent times, the number of issues on which the thinking of Soviet architects has been focused in relation to the design of theatre buildings, can, on the whole, be divided into two basic groups: on the one hand, problems concerning the architectural and spatial organisation of the theatre and, on the other, issues of the architectural design of the theatre building.

The first years devoted to designing new Soviet theatres (1929-1931) were characterised by an intensive search to find innovative spatial systems for the stage and a new organisation for the theatre. These researches were conducted mainly under the slogan of 'the mass theatre' (in the sense that a large quantity of acting personnel were on stage and also large numbers occupied the auditorium) and 'the synthetic theatre' (in the sense that all kinds of visual facilities were present within one hall). These explorations were of a very turbulent nature and produced a large quantity of projects, which were interesting, but utterly remote from any realistic possibility of execution today ...

The concepts underlying the designs were directed towards creating universal spectator complexes with the largest possible capacities (seating for 3-5,000), able simultaneously to house performances by dramatic theatres of all kinds, opera, ballet, the circus, cinema, and also mass meetings (congresses), with the potential for expanding the auditorium (seating for 8-10,000) ...

However, the demands for universality and large capacities, supported in most cases by the municipal soviets, were completely at odds with the tasks of the theatrical and operatic collectives and so had to give way to the demands for specialised types of theatre buildings.[23]

The ARU Team (Nikolai Beseda, Georgii Krutikov, Vitalii Lavrov, and Valentin Popov). The Palace of the Soviets in Moscow, Competition design (preparatory stage). Cross-sections and plans (p.136). 1931.

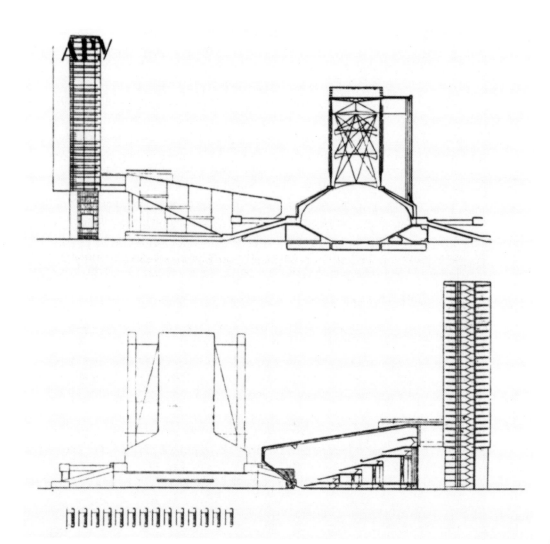

THE PALACE OF THE SOVIETS
(THE FIRST PREPARATORY PHASE OF THE COMPETITION)

The planning and founding of all possible 'Palaces' in the initial years of Soviet power reflected the proletariat's aspiration to self-affirmation as the ruling class and the desire to create a grandiose monument to the October Revolution. This found expression in a characteristic aspiration of this period – planning the 'most important building' for the country, which could become a symbol of the revolution and the new society.

Moreover, this 'most important building' was regarded as a focus for public life, as a political symbol of international importance, and even a centre for the anticipated world revolution. In the first years of Soviet power, various buildings with different purposes, based on the supposed complexity of the 'most important building's functions, were put forward to act as the country's political symbol.

A special role in planning this new type of government building and in determining an artistic image for the country's 'most important building' was played by the Competition for the Palace of the Soviets in Moscow, the three phases of which took place in the period 1931-1933. In the first, preparatory (closed) phase of the competition, during which the brief for the design was clarified, several individual architects as well as creative groups were invited to submit projects (provided by teams of their members). In all, sixteen projects were commissioned.

Architects envisaged the Palace of the Soviets not only as a place for the meetings of the country's governing bodies, with a square in front for official parades, but also as a popular forum, a place for the working masses' collective activities (demonstrations, meetings, political carnivals, spectacular military and sports displays, etc). This approach to the role of the Palace of the Soviets influenced the conception of the entire complex in most of the designs produced during the preparatory phase of the competition.

1 HALL FOR THE MASSES
2 TRIANGULAR HALL
3 EXHIBITION SPACE
4 LIBRARY
5 OFFICES
6 SCHEME FOR TRANSFORMING THE HALL FOR THE MASSES

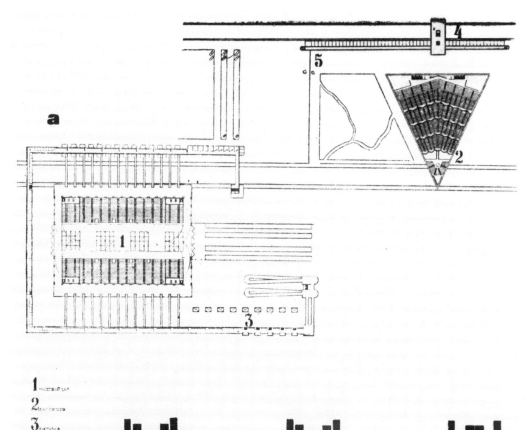

The working or business component of the Palace of the Soviets, which incorporated a small hall, was separated into an independent group of premises, subordinated compositionally to the element for mass activities, equipped with a large hall.

In their design, the team from ARU, comprising Nikolai Beseda, Georgii Krutikov, Vitalii Lavrov and Valentin Popov, conceived the Palace of the Soviets as a 'springboard for social contact among the broad working masses of the Soviet Union and a platform for the international proletariat'.

Above all, it is a propaganda centre for disseminating the principles of socialist construction among the broader masses. This aspect, which distinguishes the Palace of the Soviets from parliamentary buildings, must be developed with particular care. All the direct forms of mass propaganda must be taken into account as well as their delivery:

a) By means of the living word.
b) Through theatrical displays on the scale of mass spectacles.
c) Through various kinds of collective actions by the committed masses (demonstrations, meetings, etc); by organising exhibitions ...

In order to handle these aspects, the ARU design provides:

a) A specially developed hall for mass meetings.
b) Premises for permanent and temporary exhibitions.
c) Systems for organising the movement of masses of people (access, aisles past the tribune in the hall of the delegates, and arrangements for speeches by the masses in the hall for the masses).[24]

In the ARU team's design, the two basic groups of buildings (official and public) were clearly differentiated and spatially linked by a square for demonstrations. The official portion was conceived as a compact composition in plan, consisting of a triangular hall (for 4-5,000 people) and a high building containing offices. The basic element of the group of premises for mass activities was a large hall (for 15,000 people), which was rectangular in plan and which could be transformed (the front walls could be moved) to link it with the part of the square adjacent to it (for the deployment of mass actions), or adapted to allow the passage of demonstrations through it.

The ARU Team (Nikolai Beseda, Georgii Krutikov, Vitalii Lavrov, and Valentin Popov). The Palace of the Soviets in Moscow, Competition design (preparatory stage). Model. 1931.

...тельство

ИЗДАТЕЛЬСТВО МОСОБЛИСПОЛКОМА

Design for the cinema of Mezhrabpomfilm on Triumfalnaya Square, Moscow. Perspective. 1935.

POST-CONSTRUCTIVISM

Towards the end of 1932, there occurred an irreversible process in Soviet architecture concerning approaches to the generation of form and style. A move towards assimilating the classical heritage emerged and gained power.

In the first four or five years (1932-1936), however, this trend was still not explicitly Neo-Classical and did not entail adopting authentic details from the classical orders. In their declarations of these years, architects announced that they were not returning to the Neo-Classicism of the early twentieth century, but were simply trying to enrich the austerity of avant-garde approaches with decorative details. Using classical architectural motifs as a model, they invented new decorative elements, or added them inappropriately to architectural compositions.

This was Post-Constructivism.

In this respect, the designs for the external pavilions and the station interiors built for the first line of the Moscow Metropolitan or Metro in 1935 are typical. In these stations, the forms and details of the classical orders (pillars, pilasters, capitals, cornices, etc), were used profusely. But all these details were deliberately transformed or distorted. Architects kept their promises, as stated in their declarations, that they would assimilate the classics, but not borrow their most famous features.

This is precisely what Georgii Krutikov and Valentin Popov did in their designs for the Park of Culture (Park Kultury) Metro station. This is especially evident in the forms of the capitals used in the station's interior. They are well drawn, and their form is not really borrowed from the classics, but 'invented' anew. Equally 'invented' are other architectural forms and details on the station's façades and interiors (with the exception, perhaps, of the balusters).

This is how the authors described this station in a surviving manuscript:

> The platform hall of the station is 180 metres long and is decorated with a double row of powerful columns, faced with Crimean 'Kadikovka' marble and completed with **capitals of an original shape** [my emphasis – Khan-Magomedov].
>
> On the walls of the passages, the columns are complemented by a series of pilasters …
>
> The design envisages two painted panels on the end walls of the hall …
>
> In the above ground element of the Chudovka Street entrance hall, the design of the main staircase is reminiscent of steps in a park; it is five metres wide and leads into the station.
>
> The walls of the staircase are covered in Ural 'Ufalay' marble of grey with a blue tinge, and are designed with two rows of columns supporting the vault…
>
> On the front wall of the entrance hall, opposite the main entrance, there is space for a large painted panel …
>
> The part of the lobby that is underground serves as the ticket office, and is decorated with arcades, covered in white and grey marble …
>
> The entrance is designed as a portico with four columns of polished granite.
>
> On the façade, there is provision for sculptural decoration: 2 figures, crowning the entrance lobby, on a plinth alongside the sign 'Metro' engraved in stone, and a bas-relief above the entrance doors.

Krutikov also participated in designing stations for the second line of the Moscow Metropolitan. In 1935, he designed the interior of Revolyutsii Square, although his proposals were not used for the final building. Krutikov's design belongs to his series of Post-Constructivist projects.

Design for the interior of Revolutsii Square Metro Station on the second line of the Moscow Metropolitan. Perspective. 1935.

Georgii Krutikov and Valentin Popov. Park Kultury (Park of Culture) Metro Station on the first line of the Moscow Metropolitan. Photograph (p. 144), perspective drawing, main staircase, and the capitals on the columns. 1935.

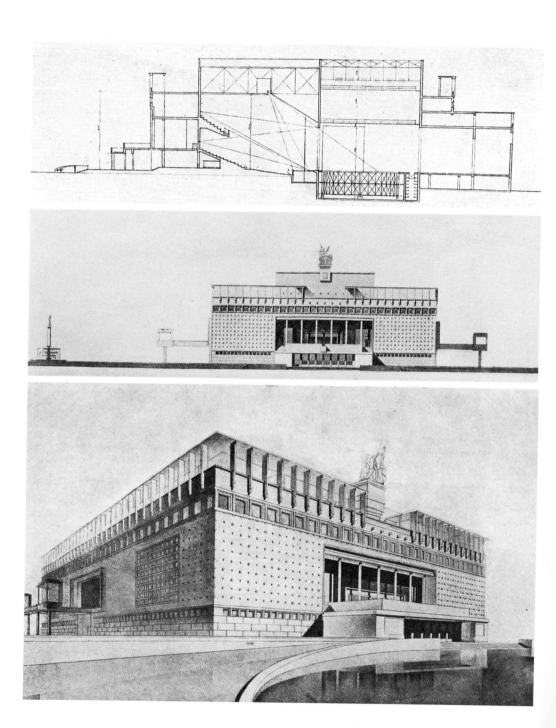

Georgii Krutikov and Valentin Popov. The Vladimir Nemirovich-Danchenko, Musical Theatre in Moscow (competition design). Cross-section, façade and perspective. 1933–1934.

Georgii Krutikov and Valentin Popov. The Vladimir Nemirovich-Danchenko, Musical Theatre in Moscow (competition design). Perspective. 1936.

His 1934 design for the cinema of the German-Russian venture Mezhrab-pomfilm (Mezhdunarodnaya rabochaya pomoshch' – film: The International Workers' Aid Film Studio) on Moscow's Triumfalnaya Square was frankly Post-Constructivist – the columns of the large and small colonnades had simplified entablatures and no capitals or plinths.

During 1935-1936, Krutikov built seven schools in various parts of Moscow, completely in the spirit of this very same Post-Constructivism. Nevertheless, the introduction of Post-Constructivist design concepts into avant-garde architecture was most evident in the competition designs for the Vladimir Nemirovich-Danchenko Musical Theatre in Moscow (architects Georgii Krutikov and Valentin Popov). Characteristically, in the distinctive architectural décor of the early projects of 1933-1934 (two variants), the architectural form of the theatre was smothered in decorative details, although amongst these details there was not one that was recognizably derived from the classical orders. All the details were 'invented'. But in the later project of 1936, the architectural form and details were already derived from the classical orders and only partially transformed.

Design for a school in Moscow.
Perspective and photograph.
1935.

THE FIGHT TO SAVE ARCHITECTURAL LANDMARKS

In the 1930s, Georgii Krutikov seems to have been very successful. Schools, residential buildings and Metro stations were all built according to his designs. The Vladimir Nemirovich-Danchenko Musical Theatre was under construction on Tverskoi Boulevard, although its completion was thwarted by the Second World War. Even so, Krutikov was not satisfied with his creative activity. Like many other Soviet architects of these years, he was unable to devote all his energies to working in the spirit of Post-Constructivism or in the Stalinist Empire style. He was not excited by the trend towards developing new forms of architectural decoration and was not inspired by design concepts that were based on assimilating the classical heritage. Although he seems to have been attracted to the problems of theatre architecture, all theatrical reforms had been suspended and the search for new forms of theatre building had been abandoned.

Klavdiya Krutikova told me in conversation that, during the second half of the 1930s, her husband suffered a creative crisis. He did not want to add to the number of classical compositions in the Stalinist Empire style. He designed and built a lot, but this did not satisfy him creatively. Krutikov's approach to architecture changed enormously towards the end of the 1930s, when during one of his trips to Kiev he met Petr Dimitrevich Baranvoskii – the legendary protector of the monuments of Russian architecture, whose uncompromising fight to preserve the country's architectural heritage made an indelible impression on Krutikov. This meeting marked the beginning of a new stage in Krutikov's career – he became involved with the problems of preserving architectural landmarks. He worked in the State Department for the Conservation of Architectural Monuments, where he had to take urgent measures. Every year, dozens of monuments were destroyed and replaced by new buildings. Objects of pre-Petrine architecture were particularly vulnerable.

The pragmatic approach to architecture, which held sway in the 1930s, was characterised not only by a disregard for inventive design, but also by an especially utilitarian attitude towards the legacy of the past. Only those architectural landmarks that related to the 'creative assimilation' of the period – and particularly to Classicism – were studied, investigated and preserved.

It seems that during the period of the Stalinist Empire style, monuments of ancient Russian architecture, especially buildings from the sixteenth to the eighteenth centuries, were not regarded as being of any great artistic value. This is the only way to explain why a whole series of great architectural landmarks from that period, which had been carefully restored in the 1920s, were demolished in the second half of the 1930s. These included the walls of Kitaiskii Gorod, the Sukharev Tower, the Golitsyn House on Okhotnyi Ryad and many others. This fate also befell many of those buildings that Krutikov had studied and tried to preserve when he was deputy head of the State Department for the Conservation of Architectural Monuments in Moscow. To a large extent, we are indebted to Krutikov for having preserved a whole series of valuable architectural complexes in Moscow. He conducted research and developed projects and proposals for including important architectural landmarks into plans for the reconstruction of Moscow. Among these were the Novospaskii Monastery; Krutitskii Yard (a group of seventeenth-century religious buildings); the cluster of buildings on Nikolskii Street (the State Printing Office and the Slavic-Greek and Latin Academy); the collection of architectural and historical monuments on Razina Street; and the seventeenth-century boyar dwelling, the manor house of the Secretary to the Duma, Averkii Kirillov, on Bersenevskaya Embankment.

A particular place in the conservation of architectural landmarks in the centre of Moscow belongs to the discovery, examination, and the plan to restore the seventeenth-century chambers in Zaryadye (April-May 1941), which had been unknown until then. This was a unique work and it established a precedent for conserving buildings of the pre-Petrine period, by freeing and purifying them of all subsequent accretions.

Krutikov used every opportunity to lobby specialists and official bodies, and consistently refused to sign documents authorising the demolition of architectural landmarks. He voiced harsh truths even when it was an occasion for congratulatory or anniversary reports. A typical example occurred on 6 July 1940, at the VII Plenum of the governing board of the Union of Soviet Architects of the USSR, which was celebrating the achievements of the fifth year of the reconstruction of Moscow. Anniversary speeches resounded from the tribune. Krutikov alone destroyed the triumphant atmosphere by sharply criticising the practice of demolishing architectural monuments *en masse*.

This is Krutikov's passionate speech to his fellow architects at the plenum:

My communication concerns the question of including valuable architectural and historical monuments in the complexes of a reconstructed Moscow and it is delivered on behalf of the Union of Soviet Architects' section for the study of Russian architecture.

The problems of reconstructing a Greater Moscow and the work of preserving historical monuments should be closely connected. Unfortunately, at the present time, people working in these two branches of one and the same enormous undertaking act completely independently of one another ... As a result, valuable buildings are being demolished. It was recently revealed by a special commission of the Academy of Architecture in Moscow that, between 1917 and 1940, 50% of the architectural and historical monuments of national Russian architecture were destroyed, and wonderful structures that were essential for studying the history and architectural talents of the Russian people were demolished. ...

... historical buildings must remain, with full rights, as living ornaments in our contemporary city. We must stop regarding them as 'disappearing Moscow'.

Here it is important to clarify the issue concerning the quantity of historical monuments. It is often necessary to argue with tendencies to artificially reduce the quantity. So, for example, it is said 'There is the Novodevichii Monastery and that is enough. The Novospaskii Monastery doesn't need to exist. There is the Kremlin and St Basils – that's enough!' It is utterly impossible to endorse this approach.

... we have at our disposal an enormous arsenal of means – both architectural and technical – to free valuable architectural landmarks from the threat of destruction and to enrich the historical appearance of the city. Here, at this plenum, we have been discussing the issue of the excessively wide streets and the immense size of the squares that have been proposed ... this excessive size is economically unprofitable for the city and it also threatens to destroy valuable architectural monuments.[25]

In one of his autobiographical notes, Krutikov wrote: 'After being demobbed in 1943, I worked in the Architectural and Planning Department of the city of Moscow, initially as an architect and then as the head of the Department for the State Conservation of Architectural Monuments in the city of Moscow. After my illness of 1950-1951, I became the deputy head of the Inspectorate for the State Conservation of Architectural Monuments in the city of Moscow.'

Krutikov's official position in the Department of the Inspectorate for the State Conservation of Architectural Monuments was such that his signature was often required to authorise the demolition of an architectural landmark. And it was practically impossible to get Krutikov's signature. This didn't suit a lot of people, including his immediate superiors, who often signed documents permitting the demolition of buildings, against Krutikov's wishes. Every time this happened, Krutikov protested violently. The authorities got fed up with this and so while he was on holiday, falsified documents, issued a reprimand, and then fired him. Krutikov started collecting documents to refute the falsified facts. In trying to attain justice, Krutikov became so upset that he fell ill and died in 1958.

As Krutikov's widow told me, she herself ended up amassing the documentation to exonerate her husband and took the file of materials to the vice-president of the Academy of Building and Architecture, Aleksandr Vlasov, asking him to vindicate her husband. Vlasov examined the material very sympathetically and agreed that Krutikov had been framed, but he refused to help in the process of rehabilitation, telling the widow that it wasn't worthwhile beginning a process to examine the legality of Krutikov's dismissal because he was already dead. He suggested that he and the widow should keep the matter between themselves. It wasn't worth involving others in this 'disagreement'. Vlasov was not concerned about the widow's desire to clear her husband's name; he didn't even really understand what it was all about.

Klavdiya Vasilevna Krutikova did not show me the documents that proved her husband's innocence – I simply believe her that Krutikov was framed. I also believe that Vlasov refused to help her. At that time, he also refused to help me publish an article in Italy about Moisei Ginzburg – a visa was required from the president of the Academy of Architecture. He approved my article, but would not issue a visa for it, and returned it to me with an official smile. We were at the opposite ends of the Academy's pecking order: he was the president and I was a young researcher. He felt himself to be at the top of the creative hierarchy and he did not want to let anyone through – Ginzburg or Krutikov. But time has operated in favour of the avant-garde. In architectural studies, Ginzburg has overtaken Vlasov. I think that after the publication of the present book, Krutikov will also 'overtake Vlasov'.

Krutikov was an original architect. He was the first to design a flying city in space. He also performed an almost heroic act, at the beginning of his creative career, when in protest against the Stalinist Empire style, he left architectural design and devoted himself completely to the worthy business of defending and rescuing the architectural legacy of the past. As the inventor of 'The Flying City' and defender of the architectural legacy, he was formally at the summit of his profession, although in the fight with the 'scum', he actually lost. This was the fate of many members of the creative avant-garde. Nevertheless, time is on their side.

NOTES

1. Private archive. Further detailed references will not be provided. All documents and quotations without specific references should be regarded as material from private archives.

2. *Spravochnik Otdela IZO Narkomprosa* (Moscow, 1920), p. 49.

3. Konstantin Tsiolkovskii (1857-1935) is one of the fathers of modern cosmonautics: in 1903 he proposed jet engines as a method of travelling outside the Earth's atmosphere.

4. *Izvestiya ASNOVA* (Moscow, 1926).

5. G. Krutikov, 'Krugloe i polukrugloe zhilishche', *Stroitel'naya promyshlennost'*, No. 9 (1927), pp. 617-618.

6. Ibid., p. 618.

7. *Arkhitektura i VKhUTEIN*, No. 1 (January 1929), p. 4.

8. G. Krutikov, 'Arkhitekturnaya nauchno-issledovatel'skaya laboratoriya', *Stroitel'naya promyshlennost'*, No. 5 (1928), p. 373.

9. *Stroitel'naya promyshlennost'*, No. 5 (1928), p. 372.

10. *Arkhitektura i VKhUTEINa*, No. 1 (Moscow, 1929), p. 2

11. Ibid.

12. For more details of these apparatus, see S.O. Khan-Magomedov, 'Psikhotekhnicheskaya laboratoriya VKhUTEINa (1927-1930)', *Tecknicheskaya estetika*, No. 1 (1978), p. 18.

13. *Arkhitektura i VKhUTEIN*, p. 2.

14. *Izvestiya* (27 May 1928).

15. *Postroika* (3 July 1928).

16. *Postroika* (12 August 1928).

17. *Sovremennaya arkhitektura*, No. 4 (1928), p. 110.

18. A. Mordvinov, 'Leonidovshchina i ee bred', *Iskusstvo v massy*, No. 12 (1930), p. 12.

19. *Stroitel'naya promyshlennost'*, No. 6-7 (1930), p. 567.

20. Albert Kelsey, *Program and Rules for the Competition for the Selection of an Architect for the Monumental Lighthouse, which the Nations of the World will Erect in the Dominican Republic to the Memory of Christopher Columbus* (Washington: Pan American Union, 1928), pp. 17-18.

21. V. Roskin, 'O Lisitskom', *Dekorativnoe iskusstvo SSSR*, No. 5 (1966), p. 28.

22. G. Krutikov, 'Voprosy prostranstvennoi organizatsii kul'turnogo kombinata i novogo teatra', *Stroitel'naya promyshlennost'*, No. 10 (1930), pp. 789-795.

23. G. Krutikov, 'Proektirovanie i stroitel'stvo teatrov v SSSR', *Arkhitektura SSSR*, No. 3 (1934), p. 8.

24. N. Beseda, G. Krutikov, V. Lavrov and V. Popov, 'Proekt brigady ARU', *Sovetskaya arkhitektura*, No. 4 (1931), pp. 45-47.

25. *Arkhitekturnye voprosy rekonstruktsii Moskvy* (Moscow, 1940), pp. 47, 48.

BIBLIOGRAPHY

Arkhitekturnyi voprosy rekonstruktsii Moskvy [Architectural Questions concerning the Reconstruction of Moscow], (Moscow, 1940).

N. Beseda, G. Krutikov , V. Lavrov and V. Popov, 'Proekt brigada ARU' [The ARU Team's Design], *Sovetskaya arkhitektura*, No. 4 (1931).

'Borba za masterstvo' [The Struggle for Mastery], *Arkhitektura SSSR*, No. 5, 1936.

'Brigada ARU. Dvorets Sovetov' [The ARU Team. The Palace of the Soviets], *Sovetskaya arkhitekura*, No. 4 (1931).

S. O. Khan-Magomdeov, 'Psikhoteknicheskaya laboratoriya VKhUTEINa (1927-1930)' [The Psycho-Technical Laboratory at the Vkhutein (1927-1930)], *Tekhnicheskaya estetika*, No. 1 (1978).

S. O. Khan-Magomdeov, 'Proekt Letayushego goroda' [The Design of 'The Flying City'], *Dekorativnoe iskusstvo*, No. 1 (1973).

S. O. Khan-Magomdeov, 'Problemy dinamicheskoi formy v tvorcheskikh kontseptsiyakh 20-kh godov' [Problems of Dynamic Form in the Creative Concepts of the 1920s], *Trudy VNIITE* (seriya *Tekhnicheskaya estetika*) No. 33 (1978).

S. O. Khan-Magomdeov, *100 shedevrov sovetskogo arkhitekturnogo avangarda* [100 Masterpieces of Soviet Avant-Garde Architecture], (Moscow, 2004).

N. Kolli, 'Arkhitektura moskovskogo metro' [The Architecture of the Moscow Metro], *Arkhitektura SSSR*, No. 4 (1935).

N. Kruglov, 'Teatr im. V. I. Nemirovicha- Danchenko. Vtoroi konkurs na proekt zdaniya' [The V. I. Nemirovich-Danchenko Theatre. The Second Competition for the Design of the Building], *Sovetskaya arkhitektura*, No. 6 (1933).

G. Krutikov, 'Krugloe i polukrugloe zhilishche' [Circular and Semi-Circular Housing], *Stroitel'naya promyshlennost'*, No. 9 (1927).

G. Krutikov, 'Arkhitekturanaya nauchno-issledovatel'skaya laboratorii pri arkhitekturnom fakul'tete Moskovsksogo vyshogo khudozhestvnno-tekhnicheskogo institute' [The Architectural Scientific and Research Laboratory in the Architecture Faculty of the Moscow Higher Artistic and Technical Institute], *Stroitel'naya promyshlennost'*, No. 5 (1928).

G. Krutikov, 'Arkhitekturanaya nuchno-issledovatel'skaya laboratoriya pri arkhitekturnom fakul'tete VKhUTEINa. Rabota laboratoriya 1928/1929 uchebnom godu' [The Architectural Scientific and Research Laboratory in the Architecture Faculty of the Vkhutein. The Laboratory's Work during the Academic Year 1928-1929], *Arkhitekura i VKhUTEIN*, No. 1 (January 1929).

G. Krutikov, 'Voprosy prostranstvennoi organizatsii kul'turnogo kombinata i novogo teatra' [Questions Concerning the Spatial Organisation of the Cultural Complex and the New Theatre], *Stroitel'naya promyshlennost'*, No.10 (1930).

G. Krutikov, 'Voprosy prostranstvennoi organizatsii kul'turnogo kombinata' [Questions Concerning the Spatial Organisation of the Cultural Complex], *Stroitel'naya promyshlennost'*, No. 2-3 (1931).

G. Krutikov, 'Voprosy obshchestvenno-prostranstvennoi organizatsii poseleniya posledovatel'no sotsialistichogo tipa. Gorod-kommuna "Avtostroi"' [Questions Concerning the Social and Spatial Organisation of a Consistently Socialist Type of Settlement. The Town-Commune 'Avtostroi'], *Sovetskaya arkhitektura*, No. 1-2 (1931).

G. Krutikov, 'Bol'shoi Sintekticheskii teatr v Sverdlovske' [The Great Synthetic Theatre in Sverdlovsk], *Sovetskaya arkhitektura*, No. 1 (1932).

G. Krutikov, 'Proektirovanie i stroitel'stvo teatrov v SSSR' [The Design and Construction of Theatres in the USSR], *Arkhitektura SSSR*, No. 3 (1934).

V. Lavrov, 'Iz poslednikh rabot Arkhitekturnogo fakulteta VKhUTEINa' [The Most Recent Work of the Vkhutein's Architecture Faculty], *Stroitel'stvo Moskvy*, No. 10 (1928).

N. Levochskii, 'Sovetskie zhiul-verny. VKhUTEMAS gotovit ne stroitelei a fatazeistov. Proekt postroiki "Letayushego goroda"' [Soviet Jules Vernes. The Vkhutemas is not Training Builders but Day-Dreamers. The Construction Project 'The Flying City'], *Postroika* (3 July 1928).

Prezidium arkhitekturnogo fakul'teta VKhUTEINa, 'My gotovim ne "sovetskie zhyul'-vernov". Arkhitekturnyi fakul'tet na dolzhnoi vysote' [We are not training 'Soviet Jules Vernes'. The Architecture Faculty is on the Correct Path], *Postroika* (12 August 1928).